MASS MEDIA CHRISTIANITY

TELEVANGELISM AND THE GREAT COMMISSION

BY
JERRY D. CARDWELL

With Contributions by
JACK L. THORPE

Afterword by THE REVEREND JOHN LOVING
Rector, Grace Episcopal Church
Ponca City, Oklahoma

UNIVERSITY
PRESS OF
AMERICA

LANHAM • NEW YORK • LONDON

Copyright © 1984 by

University Press of America,™ Inc.

4720 Boston Way
Lanham, MD 20706

3 Henrietta Street
London WC2E 8LU England

Library of Congress Cataloging in Publication Data

Cardwell, J.D. (Jerry Delmas)
  Mass media Christianity.

  Bibliography: p.
  Includes index.
  1. Mass media in religion—United States. 2. Televi-
sion in religion—United States. 3. Evangelists—United
States. 4. Evangelicalism—United States. I. Thorpe,
Jack L. II. Title. III. Title: Televangelism and the
great commission.
BV652.95.C365   1984   269'.2'0973   84-19519
ISBN 0-8191-4323-5 (alk. paper)
ISBN 0-8191-4324-3 (pbk. : alk. paper)

For my Mother, Jimmie Hester Cardwell, and my Father,
    Lupton Delmas Cardwell. May the great reward be
    theirs.

iv

ACKNOWLEDGEMENTS

Intellectual debts are not legal tender and, therefore, cannot be repaid. Although they cannot be repaid, intellectual debts can be acknowledged. The only problem with acknowledging intellectual debts is the danger of failing, innocently, to mention someone who should be mentioned. I hope I do not make that mistake.

Dr. James W. Grimm and Dr. Louis M. Beck spent much of their valuable time reading the manuscript in different states of completion and polish. Dr. H. Kirk Dansereau, Dr. Tom Dunn and Dr. Paul Wozniak also read portions of the manuscript. Everyone who read the manuscript, or portions thereof, made many useful and constructive comments on the material they reviewed. I must say that I did not take all of their advice; perhaps I should have done so-- the book may have been better for it.

My wife of 20 years, Nancy, read, and reread the manuscript in her usual, thorough way. In her own way, she kept dragging me back toward the middle ground of objectivity. If I have drifted to far from objectivity, it is not because I was not forewarned.

My two sons, Robert Michael and Jonathon Alexander, have surrendered the television to my viewing needs over, and over again. Both Robert and Jonathon have watched the T.V. preachers with me on many occasions. It may very well be that their insights, the insights of children, were the most instructive of all.

I would also like to express my thanks to the parishioners of Christ Episcopal Church, Bowling Green, Kentucky, for permitting me to teach Church School on the subject of Christian television. They sat politely for three Sundays, and listened; in so doing they allowed me to hear what I was writing. I recommend such a process to clear one's thinking and sharpen one's focus.

The Reverend John H. Loving, Rector of Grace Episcopal Church in Ponca City, Oklahoma, agreed to write the Afterword to the book. His words are reasoned, humble, and yet forceful. The Reverend Loving's "response" is exactly what I anticipated from such an intelligent and sincere man of God. His thoughts are truly appreciated.

Finally, I would be remiss if I did not thank the T.V. preachers for being so persistent in coming into my home. Without them, the book would not have been written. I invite the reader to put the accuracy of what I have said in these pages to the test by watching Christian television. It can't hurt, it might help, and the uninitiated will certainly learn something about an important social movement in American society.

Jerry D. Cardwell
Bowling Green, Ky
June, 1984

MASS MEDIA CHRISTIANITY: TELEVANGELISM AND THE GREAT
COMMISSION

TABLE OF CONTENTS

PREFACE

Religion is at once the most normative and the most
problematic of human institutions. No other area of
human life is quite as capable of stirring the
imagination or the emotions as is religion. Because of
its position of centrality in guiding the moral conduct
of everyday human affairs, religion has proven to be
both comforting and offensive in American society. A
religious person may be comforted by his own religious
beliefs, but offended by the beliefs of others. The
unbeliever may be comforted by no religious beliefs,
and offended by all of them. Regarding religion, it is
difficult to suspend judgement and occupy a neutral
ground in our society.

Religion has traditionally been most problématic
during times of religious renewal or revival in
American society. We are in the throes of such a time
today. The primary difference between past religious
revivals and the revival of today, however, is
visibility. Today, the religious revival is taking
place before our very eyes, on television. No longer
are the revivals restricted to the local church, the
local football stadium, or a camp-meeting tent. Today,

the preachers of the Gospel bring their religious message to our living rooms, our dens, and our bedrooms. Through the technology of television, religion is being thrust into the forefront of the public imagination. This very visibility portends a renewal and revival unlike those in the recent history of our society. The visibility also guarantees, we believe, that the container of human imagination and emotion will be stirred in a way unique in America. One will not be able to simply sit and watch the drama take place as T.V. religion moves to "bring America back to her `proper' religious foundations, and her religious senses."

That there is a new religious revival in America has been, and is, well documented. With the twin powers of the television and the computer, however, this revival will be unlike any other we have witnessed. While the traditional, mainline faiths will benefit from the religious awakening, the fuel that feeds the force of the movement will come largely from the evangelicals and the television church. In fact, the T.V. church will not only supply some of the fuel, it will be an important force behind the new revival.

In addition to television and computers, the T.V. ministers are well aware of the potential that the communication satellites have for impacting the lives of people over the whole planet. Today they have broadcasts reaching not only Americans, but people in Europe, Asia, Africa, Australia, and Central America. Indeed, they reach almost every corner of the earth. The growing influence of the T.V. preachers in speaking to the consciousness of people is not confined to America. The Mass Media Ministers are working hard to fulfill the "great commission"; they are working hard "to save the world."

In writing this book, we have made no attempt to insult, ridicule, or otherwise negatively characterize the T.V. preachers. In testimony to this, we made the first two chapters of the book available to Jim Bakker's PTL ministries in early 1984, including a copy to Mr. Bakker. Along with the first two chapters we requested that the PTL organization review the material and let us know their thoughts on what we were saying, and how we were saying it. Two executives of PTL told us they would be pleased to review the material and appreciated the opportunity to do so; alas, no one at

PTL ever responded.

The reader will note that the book contains a response from a representative of the mainline church. We feel we should point out that we offered Jim Bakker, Jerry Falwell, and Zola Levitt the opportunity to include a response as a representative of the T.V. preachers. Bakker's ministry never responded, Falwell's representative said he was to busy, and Levitt's ministries also indicated that Mr. Levitt was unable to write a response. Mention is made of these facts in order to point out that every effort was made to be open and forthright about the book, and to maintain objectivity and balance. We made the opportunities to respond available but the T.V. preachers we contacted decided not to do so.

With these things in mind, we have undertaken to write a book concerning what Hadden and Swann have called the "Prime Time Preachers," and what we call the "Mass Media Ministers." It is our hope that after reading the book the reader will have a better understanding of the power, influence, and potential for social change that is embodied in Mass Media Christianity. We would also hope that after reading this book some people will take the time to watch some of the programs that are telecast on the Electronic Church, and make up their own minds about the significance of this movement for the future of socio-religious problems in American society. The reader who does watch the T.V. preachers should keep in mind that these people are reaching out to scores of countries. The "hook" has been baited, and the T.V. preachers are getting their catch. What will be done with the catch is worthy of thought, and perhaps, action.

Jerry D. Cardwell
Bowling Green, KY

ART
ACKNOWLEDGEMENTS

The author wishes to express his appreciation to Mr.
John Warren Oakes, associate professor of art, Western
Kentucky University, for permission to reproduce his
renderings of several Mass Media Ministers. Dr. Oakes'
work appears in Chapters Four and Five, and his drawings
represent an important contribution in their own right.

THE   ADVENT: PREPARING   THE   WAY   FOR   MASS   MEDIA
CHRISTIANITY

THE ADVENT: PREPARING THE WAY FOR MASS MEDIA CHRISTIANITY

Let no man deceive himself. If any man
among you seemeth to be wise in this world,
let him become a fool, that he may be wise.
For the wisdom of this world is foolishness
with God.

I Cor. 3:18-19

INTRODUCTION

How and why are people religious? To understand being
religious or being a religious person,we will examine
the idea of religious commitment; an idea that has been
central to much of the sociology of religion for the
past twenty-five years. For those who are not familiar
with the language of sociology, we point out that the
terms religious commitment, religiosity, and
religiousness are used interchangeably in this book. We
have limited ourselves to the past twenty-five years in
full awareness that religious commitment has been a
meaningful idea in the sociology of religion for a much
longer period of time.1 But renewed interest in
religiousness began in the early 1960's, and has
occupied much of center stage since that time. Today, a
comprehensive book in the sociology of religion must,
it seems, devote a substantial portion of its

discussion to the idea of religious commitment.2

When sociologists address the notion of religiousness we do not have reference to what it "means" to be religious. We do have reference to the ways in which people are and can be religious, for as regards this question the answer resides in the extent of our ability to develop new, or at least different, categories to study religiosity. Sociologists, anthropologists, psychologists, and others have struggled and agonized over the "meaning" of religious commitment since the beginning of their disciplines. As yet, no satisfactory answer has been forthcoming. Today we know more of the neurotic, the psychotic, the deviant, the corporate, and the political personality than we know of the religious personality. This is not to argue that we are incapable of studying religiousness; we can study, but we cannot, or more precisely have not, grasped what it "means" to be religious in any theological sense. Thus, our concern in this chapter is not with the "meaning" of religious commitment, but rather with differences in religious commitment as they are revealed in the many and diverse methods that have been devised to measure religiousness. We leave the discussion of "meaning" to those who argue late into the night and seldom arrive at mutually satisfactory conclusions. We discuss "traditional" modes of religious commitment because in order to understand the peculiar attraction of Christian television, we must first understand the historical ways of studying religious commitment and religious involvement.

FROM SIMPLICITY TO DIVERSITY: RELIGIOUSNESS IN REVIEW

Because the foolishness of God is wiser then men,
and the weakness of God is stronger than men.

I Corinthians 1:25

Historically, when sociologists have undertaken to study religious commitment, they have used rather

2

simple measures such as church attendance (participation), affiliation, or an expressed belief in God or Jesus. Examples of the former are found throughout the sociological literature with one of the most celebrated being Joseph Fichter's fourfold characterization of church participants as (1) dormant, (2) marginal, (3) modal, or (4) nuclear church members.3 For Fichter, degree of religious commitment was based on participation in prescribed rituals (mass, confession, communion, and parochial education for children), participation in the organization of the church, and degree of interest expressed in the church. The people Fichter characterized as "dormant" members did nothing more than acknowledge their church membership, while "marginal" members met some (but not many) of the prescribed requirements. The "dormant" and "marginal" members would correspond to what sociologists call people who are "low" in religious commitment. On the other hand, the "modal" and "nuclear" members were those who met, and/or exceeded, all minimal requirements and, accordingly, were classified as "high" in religious commitment. Allen Spitzer followed a pattern similar to Fichter's, in which Roman Catholics were classified as (1) formal Catholics, (2) nominal Catholics, (3) cultural Catholics, and (4) folk Catholics.4 Similar measures have been developed for Mormons, Lutherans, and Episcopalians.5

It is true that these efforts were primarily concerned with assessing "types" of church members; nevertheless, in other studies the same measures have also been used as measures of religiosity. What frequently happens, even if other measures of religiousness are used, is that those who score high on a given measure are characterized as nuclear, or modal (or both), and those who score low are discussed as marginal, or dormant (or both). It is clear that Fichter's classification of types of church members is based on participation and is, at a minimum, a substitute measure of religious commitment based on affiliation and attendance.

Measures of religious commitment based on participation, affiliation, or a belief in God, leave as many questions unanswered as they answer. While they permit us to characterize people as to "types of church members," they leave unanswered questions relating to variations between religious groups regarding traditional participation patterns. It is well documented, for example, that Catholics attend more frequently than Protestants or Jews, and that Protestants attend more frequently than Jews.6. Such data raise the question of whether "dormant" means the same thing for Catholics as it does for Jews or Protestants. Even beyond frequency of attendance is the question of regularity of attendance. It may be that over an extended period of time the regular, but less frequent attender may be more consistently involved in the church than is the frequent, but more erratic attender. Frequency of attendance and regularity of attendance are dissimilar behaviors and may mean quite different things.

Associated with the problem of "types of members," is the problem of explanation of level of participation. Should we reasonably classify the physically immobile, the sick, those who work on the worship day, and similar persons as low in religiousness? It should be recognized that there are a variety of reasons for attending or not attending church. Members of an ecclesia may attend church frequently for reasons quite different than members of a sect, and members of a sect may attend for reasons substantially different from members of an established denomination. Persons may attend because attendance is "good business," that is, it is good to be "seen in church." Attendance may simply be an internalized habit, or viewed as a duty or obligation.7 Certainly, the church member may attend church because of a deep and abiding desire to worship God; or the perceived need for spiritual or other help may be an important factor in the decision to attend church.

Equally important is the realization that a concern with "types of participation" does not provide information concerning why people do not attend church. The unanswered question is why those who do not attend (as well as those who do), choose one course of conduct over another. What is the likelihood that non-attenders can be classified by the legitimacy of their motives for not attending church? Is an important factor the inability to influence important decisions made in the church, or limited family time, or occupational obligations, or dislike for a pastor, or a belief that the church is not adequately involved in community affairs? Is nonattendance made acceptable by a belief that organized religion is unimportant, or only just

4

one more social organization? It seems reasonable to suggest that church members who are classified as low in religious commitment may have acceptable motives for their nonattendance and may, in reality, be more religious than their counterparts who attend frequently and are labeled as being "high" in religiosity. Glenn Vernon has conducted research that shows that nonaffiliates-- what he called religious "nones" --also show significant variation in religiousness.8

Finally, we must point out that the various characterizations of "types" of church members may, in fact, omit more than they include. We say this because of the rather obvious point that the idea of "types" characterizes people only in regard to organized, church religion.9 As a result, large segments of the population are not even considered as regards their type of religious participation. The author has been engaged in a content analysis of Pat Robertson's "700 Club," Jim Bakker's "PTL Club," and Jerry Falwell's "Old Time Gospel Hour,"and we have been intrigued with the possibility and probability that perhaps thousands of the viewers of these Christian television programs are nominally members of a local congregation but are content to receive their religion via Christian television.10 These people, who may be classified, on the basis on nonattendance at church, as "low" in their personal religiousness, may also be equally or more pious than others who are classified as "high" in religiosity because they frequently attend worship services at a church. In recent broadcasts of the "PTL Club" and Dr. John Hash's "News of the World and the Word," the established churches have been attacked as the "enemies of the Body of Christ." Some, perhaps many, viewers of Christian television may accept such pronouncements and choose nonaffiliation but, nevertheless, be highly religious. Again, Vernon's research on religious "nones" clearly shows neglect of these people to be an important mistake.11

Whatever the shortcomings, use of church attendance and/or participation has long been a measure of religious commitment in sociology. Even though such measures may obscure as much as they reveal, often failing to illustrate variations that exist within as well as between religions, they have proven useful in demonstrating attitude and behavioral differences in different religious groups. Such secular areas as attitudes toward work, political party preference,

pre-marital and extra-marital sex, attitudes toward
abortion, and others, have been shown to be related to
frequency of church attendance. While it is simple, the
characterization of people into "types of members" does
have its benefits in assessing religiousness.12

A second area of measurement in religious commitment
has focused on beliefs and rituals. We will now turn
our attention to those two areas of religiousness.

RELIGIOUS COMMITMENT: ATTACHMENT TO BELIEFS AND
PERFORMANCE OF RITUALS

You shall have no other Gods before me

Deuteronomy 5:7

Observe the Sabbath day by keeping it holy, as the Lord
your God has commanded you

Deuteronomy 5:12

We know of no sociologists who would disagree with
the position that religions expect their adherents to
accept certain minimum beliefs, or with the idea that
participation in certain rituals is also normally
expected. In the Christian heritage, we have in mind
such beliefs as a belief in God, belief in the Divinity
of Jesus Christ, life after death, the resurrection of
Jesus, and so forth. In Islam, the believer is expected
to believe in only one God (Allah), and to believe that
Mohammed was a prophet of God to whom Allah revealed
the Koran. Whatever the religion-- Judaism,
Christianity, Islam, Hinduism, Buddhism, Jainism,
Confucianism, or Taoism --there are certain minimum
beliefs expected of professing followers.

Just as they are expected to accept certain beliefs,
religious persons are also expected to perform certain
rituals on a regular basis, and often at specified
times. For example, Christians are expected to attend

6

the regularly scheduled worship services, to pray, to receive Holy Communion, and so on. Islamic adherents, on the other hand, are expected to bow toward Mecca at the specified five times each day. Jews should abstain from pork and study Torah with consistency and awe. Some religious groups prescribe avoidance behavior, while others indicate what sorts of conduct are to be undertaken frequently and with regularity. Whatever the form of ritual activity, participation in ritual is normatively expected of religious followers

As the reader might suspect, there are many difficulties associated with the study of religious commitment through an assessment of personal attachment to religious beliefs. The precariousness of measuring religiousness in this way can most readily be illustrated by an examination of responses to questions about "belief in God." For example, when national samples of people are asked "Do you believe in God," 85 to 90 percent consistently answer with an unequivocal "yes." What does such an answer mean? Do all of those people affirming a belief in God believe in God in the same way? We need to ask what such an answer tells us insofar as religious commitment is concerned. Demerath and Levinson have done research which shows that all of the people who say they do believe in God do not conceive of God in the same way.13 They studied a sample of university students by asking whether they believed in God, and 86 percent answered affirmatively. The same students were then asked to pick one of five statements concerning God that came closest to their own conception, and forty-six percent choose statements that were agnostic or nonorthodox. In their research dealing with the relationship between self-esteem and God image, Benson and Spilka found a significant relationship between these two variables. Based on their study of a sample of 128 Catholic subjects "with approximately identical religious backgrounds," Benson and Spilka found that "self esteem was positively related to loving-accepting God-images and negatively to rejecting images."14 In essence, these researchers found that as personal self-esteem increased, individuals were much more likely to view God as a loving God. Clearly, a simple "yes" to a query concerning belief in God is not very informative. As Demerath and Hammond have suggested, a "yes" answer "may mean only that more than nine out of ten [people] answer questions from strangers so as to avoid the stigma of a nonconformist, atheistic no."15 It is undoubtedly true that there are a variety of ways to believe in God.

A similar problem relates to the belief in Jesus Christ. Does the person believe that Jesus was only a man, although an extraordinary one; a great man and very holy; that Jesus is basically Divine; or that Jesus is the Divine Son of God with no doubts about it? Any one of these positions may be represented in a "yes" response to the question, "Do you believe in Jesus?" In some of our own research, we have found that among those who "believe in Jesus," 60 percent thought him to be the Divine Son of God with no doubts, 28 percent believed him to be a great and holy man, but not Divine, and eight percent thought of Jesus as only a man.16 Information from France indicates a similar pattern.17 When Catholics were asked to answer the question "To You, Christ is," seven percent answered "a Person out of a Legend," nine percent "a Philosopher whose ideas have been taken over and are today outdated," 17 percent "a man whose moral doctrine is still valid today," 51 percent "The Son of God," nine percent "a prophet," and seven percent "Don't know." Again, a "yes" answer to a simple question about belief in Jesus camouflages as much as it reveals.

An examination of the performance of ritual reveals many of the same problems which are associated with an analysis of belief. For example, "Congregationalists are least orthodox in doctrine and belief, poorest attenders of religious services, poorest givers (despite being second only to Episcopalians in median income), and most socially-ethically concerned." Based on good evidence supplied by a number of sociologists, Donald Ploch has reached the following conclusions:18

> For the most part, means [of religious participation] move in a steady progression from Congregational through Episcopalian, Methodist, Presbyterian, American Baptist, Lutheran (American, then Missouri Synod), Southern Baptist, to sectarian, Roman Catholics are in general a little more orthodox, better attenders, better givers, and less socially-concerned than the average Protestant. However, the Protestant-Catholic difference is now as large as the Congregational-Southern Baptist one.

What all of this suggests is that questions designed to measure religious ritualism may tell us about rates of involvement, but may not be providing much or meaningful information concerning intensity or saliency of ritual participation in religiosity.19

INDIVIDUAL RELIGIOSITY AND THE CHURCH ANALOGY

Again, whey you pray, do not be like the hypocrites; they love to say their prayers standing up in synagogue and at the street-corners, for everyone to see them. I tell you this: they have their reward already.

Matthew 6:5

The measures of religiousness we have discussed thus far are attempts to study individual religiosity. It is true that almost all such efforts refer to commitment to what has been called "Church Religion"; nevertheless, our measures have dealt with individual commitment to church religion. We mention this because, like other sociologists, we have been quoted as saying that "based on our research, one group is more religious than another." Of course, that is simply not true; we have never claimed that one religious group is more devout than another. It is easy, however, to see how lay persons, and even sociologists, could reach such a conclusion.

The measures we have been discussing to this point, and many of those we will discuss later, tell us how frequently a person attends church, takes Holy Communion, contributes financially to the church, and/or prays; they also provide information about acceptance of the belief of a given religious group. However, these measures tell us nothing about corporate, or organizational religious commitment, precisely because organizations, as such, are not religiously committed. We can, and do, convert attendance and belief statistics into rates; but again, these rates in no way tell us that one religion is more religious than another religion. It is true, for example, that Southern Baptists attend worship services

9

more frequently than Episcopalians, and that Mormons attend more frequently than Southern Baptists. But this kind of evidence does not support a conclusion that the Southern Baptist church is more religious than the Episcopal church, or that the Mormon church is more religious than the Southern Baptist church. In point of fact, such evidence does not support a conclusion that an individual of one church is more or less religious than an individual of another church. All that these data tell us is that the Mormon person is likely to attend more frequently than the Southern Baptist person.

If we take Paul Tillich's notion of faith as "ultimate concern" as a benchmark over against which we will evaluate the degree, or level of religiosity, then we must know the centrality of participation and belief as we attempt to address even individual religiosity.20 It seems reasonable to assume that there are persons who never attend worship services but who, nevertheless, are very religious. The nonparticipant may, we would want to argue, have had several confirming encounters with God and/or Jesus. It may very well be that such a person does not believe church attendance to be part of what Tillich has called the "centered act of faith." Yet, on the other hand, it seems equally reasonable to suggest that it is possible for attendance and/or involvement in liturgy to be believed to be a vital part of the "centered act of faith." It seems to us that an important component of religious commitment is missing in much of our data on this question. Keeping in mind that we are not searching for the theological "meaning" of religiousness; we are, nevertheless, not relieved of the responsibility of concerning ourselves with the question of the centrality of a particular act or belief. By "centrality" we mean to ask whether the act or conduct in question is important to the person as regards their view of what counts for religiousness. A person may consider her or himself religious because they view attendance or participation in liturgy as central to religiousness, or they may not. That, of course, is an empirical question that begs, still today, for an answer.

In much of the research and writing on individual religiousness, the individual's own view of his or her religiousness is completely ignored. What we have reference to is the idea that the person's self concept is a multidimensional phenomenon, with one of the dimensions corresponding to how the person views him or herself in religious terms; in other words, their religious self concept. We have already pointed out that a person's self esteem is significantly related to their image of God. One thing this research does not tell us is that low self esteem people are less religious than high self esteem people. The research does tell us that low and high self esteem persons are different-- different in regard to how they conceive of God. Perhaps they are also different with respect to whether they consider themselves to be religious.

As most readers are aware, self concepts involve the process of attributing a definition of oneself to oneself. The fact that religion has been such a persistent and important element in American society is sufficient to conclude that it would be extremely difficult for an individual to exist in our society without religion influencing, in some way, his or her self concept. Now the fact that religion does influence self concepts allows at least two possible ways of viewing oneself relative to religion: (1) one may define him or herself as in harmony with the standards set by religion, or (2) one may define him or herself as at variance with religious standards. Given this, we believe we need to begin to direct much more attention to an analysis of religious self definitions. It is important to document, and to begin to understand, that there are those who provide little evidence of commitment to church religion but who, nevertheless, consider themselves to be very religious.

SOCIAL CHANGE AND RELIGION

Behold, I come quickly: blessed is he
that keepeth the sayings of the prophecy
of this book.

Revelation 22:7

   As almost any observer of social life can tell us,

America is a rapidly changing society. While social scientists have known this truism for a long time, Alvin Toffler popularized it and brought it into the forefront of the public imagination in his best selling book, Future Shock. It seems that things are always changing in the United States. This is true of politics, of the economy, of education, of the family, and it is certainly true of religion. In the pages that follow, we will focus our attention on changes that have occured, are occuring, and on those changes we believe will occur, in one of the most fascinating and controversial areas of human social life-- religion.

Perhaps no other area stirs the emotions and arouses the passions of people more than does religion. This is true, we think, for those who are religious, and equally true for those who are not. It is no accident that the Judeo-Christian tradition of this society provides the fulcrum upon which the moral authority of our conduct is balanced. This has been historically true, and it remains true today. It remains true in spite of the outcries that America is becoming a "god-less" society.

Not long ago the author of this book was the Director of the Center for Research on Religiosity at a small college in Virginia. On one occasion he was interviewed by the Richmond Times-Dispatch newspaper concerning the current state of religion in America.21 The interview took place during a very unstable time in American society. In that interview, the author expressed the view that religion, like other institutions, was experiencing a "crisis in faith"; that is, church members were losing their faith in the institution of religion. The reasons were defined as being many and complex. Two, however, seemed to stand out.

THE CHARISMA OF THE OBSCURE

    And the multitudes that went before,
and that followed, cried, saying, Hosanna
to the son of David: Blessed is he that
cometh in the name of the Lord; Hosanna
in the highest. And when he was come into
Jerusalem, all the city was moved, saying, Who is this?

Matthew 21:9-10

First, it seemed that religion no longer was the primary source of meaning for society for what was to be considered the "moral," the "just," or the "right" in human affairs. In fact, it seemed then, and it seems today, that society has become the primary informer of religion as to what is right, moral, or acceptable. The consequences of this shift are many, although one seems most important. To the extent that religion has changed from informing society to being informed by society, the eternal values of religion must be called into question. It is precarious, at best, to provide alternative interpretations to eternal values; it is disastrous to change them in order to keep pace with secular social change. One effect is that religion looses what Thomas O'Dea has called the " charisma of the obscure."22 What O'Dea meant by the "charisma of the obscure" is the ability of the sacred or holy, of the unusual and the powerful, to inspire awe, respect, and fascination in people. As long as religion possesses this quality it possesses the "charisma of the obscure," and the ability to inspire and direct human affairs. When it loses this quality, in any degree, it risks becoming mundane and pedestrian and, simultaneously, losing its ability to inspire awe, reverence, and obedience in people. If one needs evidence to support the importance of maintaining the "charisma of the obscure," one need only look at the phenomenal growth of the fundamentalist churches, and the corresponding drop in membership of the moderate to liberal churches that have tried to "adapt to a changing society."

We might ask why the fundamentalist churches have grown and continue to grow. In answering such a question we can provide many answers; one, however, seems to stand out in our minds. These churches-- Assemblies of God, Church of the Nazarene, Seventh Day Adventist, Southern Baptist-- have refused to compromise their basic theology in order to keep pace with rapidly changing societal values. These churches, along with other pentecostal, charismatic, and holiness faiths, emphasize being "born again," speaking in tongues, physical and spiritual healing by faith, and being infilled or annointed with the Holy Spirit. Consider, on the other hand, what the Protestant

Episcopal Church has done in recent years. To begin, it has recently revised, and put into the everyday English, its Book of Common Prayer. In addition, it has voted in favor of the ordination of women, and has raised the possibility of ordaining homosexuals. In some of our own research in a large Episcopal Diocese, less than one-half of the Episcopal ministers we asked indicated that they accepted the belief that Jesus is the Divine Son of God. So what has happened to the Protestant Episcopal Church in the United States? It has lost a higher percentage of its membership than any other mainline Protestant church.

Our point is this: those faiths which have doggedly refused to dilute the basic theology of their faith, either by word or deed, have grown, while those churches that either appear to have, or actually have diluted their basic theology, have suffered losses. When the "charisma of the obscure" is compromised, the unique power of religion to attract and hold people is also compromised.

DEMYTHOLOGIZING THE FAITH

Then Jesus sent the multitude away,
and went into the house: and his disciples
came unto him, saying, Declare unto us the
parable of the tares of the field.

Matthew 13:36

A second reason that many church members have had a "crisis in faith" relative to religious institutions has to do with the process of "demythologizing" the faith. This is closely related to, but different from, loosing the "charisma of the obscure." To "demythologize" the faith means to make it less complex or less ambiguous. In other words, to make the faith less difficult to understand. This, it seems to us, is one outcome of such efforts as Vatican II, the revision of the Book of Common Prayer, and of translating the Bible into the everyday vernacular. To take away the complexity and ambiguity of religion is to remove much

14

of its power to attract followers. It is difficult, at best, to become emotionally charged or spiritually involved in something that seems perfectly clear, completely usual, and easily within the grasp of rational understanding.

In a recent article in which he was reflecting on his earlier book entitled Wayward Shepherds, published in 1971, the sociologist Rodney Stark commented that:23

> Given a choice between the living rituals of the National Football League and the demythologized rituals of leading liberal denominations, many people sensibly have opted for the former. Or, if it is religion they seek, they have turned to denominations that still possess the authentic product.

We wholeheartedly agree with Stark, but we would want to add that in addition to turning to "denominations that still possess the authentic product," many people have also turned to Christian television.

A pop version of the Wayward Shepherd findings on "sermon topics" was published in Psychology Today magazine, in 1970. This version was entitled "Sounds of Silence." Musing on his article in Psychology Today, Stark recalls that the "silence made so much of in that article [in 1970] concerned the failure of the theologically conservative clergy to devote whole sermons to secular concerns (especially to the Vietnam War)." Ten years later, in 1980, Stark reflects on his work and suggests that he failed to mention the most significant "sounds of silence"-- what he calls the "silence of profound importance," in that article. What is the "silence of profound importance" to which Stark refers? It is nothing less than the "silence about religion among the most liberal clergy."24

Stark raises the same question we are raising in this chapter on preparing the way for Mass Media Christianity: "Can faiths that discard the supernatural elements of religion function any longer as religious?" We think not, and, moreover, we are of the opinion that the T.V. preachers are among the many people who recognized the loss of the religious in the traditional, institutional church. As we shall see, if the message of T.V. religion is nothing else, it is supernatural-- it is unabashedly religious.

ON PREPARING THE WAY

Ask, and it shall be given to you; seek,
and ye shall find; knock, and it shall be
opened unto you.

Matthew 7:7

There are, of course, many more reasons that can
be provided as explanations for the "crisis in faith"
over religious institutions in America. We are
certainly aware that we have discussed only two of the
many reasons and, it is entirely possible that many
people will disagree with us regarding the importance
of those reasons. Be that as it may, one thing is
certain, the "faith crisis" is with us. The reader
should, however, be cautioned. We are not saying that
the "crisis in faith" means that America is becoming
less religious, or that America is becoming a "godless"
nation. On the contrary, we will suggest in Chapter Two
that personal religiousness (as opposed to
institutional religiousness) is on the upswing in
modern America.

Nothing, or at least almost nothing, happens
overnight. In human societies, social change is a
process, often beginning in almost undetectable ways.
Quite often, things that are done to preserve
continuity have the effect of disrupting the very
traditions which are trying to be maintained. As Peter
L. Berger has reminded us, nothing new, novel, or
unusual, will happen until other occurrences make
possible the imagining of the new, the novel, or the
unusual.25 In other words, the "crisis in faith" about
the religious institution is an outgrowth of other
societal events in America. The "crisis" did come, and
we now turn our attention to a brief discussion of the
events which made it possible, or perhaps, made it
inevitable. Later in this book we will examine some of
the consequences of this "crisis."

HUMAN INSTITUTIONS: A CRISIS IN FAITH

Behold, I stand at the door, and knock: if any
man hear my voice, and open the door, I will
come in to him, and will sup with him, and he
with me. To him that overcometh will I grant
to sit with me on my throne, even as I also
overcame, and am set down with my father in his
throne. He that hath an ear, let him hear what
the Spirit saith unto the churches.

Revelation 3:20-22

Many events have rocked our society in the past
twenty-five years; events that affected the entire
social order. We need only to consider a few of the
events of the 1960's to make our point. Consider, if
you will, the following events of the decade of the
60's:26

> 1. A Roman Catholic is elected President of
> the United States and is subsequently shot to
> death in Dallas, Texas;
>
> 2. The construction of the Berlin Wall and
> the ill-fated Bay of Pigs invasion;
>
> 3. The tremendous growth of the Civil Rights
> Movement, including sit-ins, freedom riders,
> bombings, murders of civil rights workers,
> the March on Washington, and the passage of
> the Civil Rights Act in 1964;
>
> 4. The assassinations of Martin Luther King,
> Jr., Malcolm X, and Robert Kennedy;
>
> 5. The societal wide anti-Viet Nam protests;
>
> 6. The beginnings of the women's liberation
> movement;
>
> 7. The rise of the counterculture, with its
> search for alternative life styles, including
> drug use, communal living, and the rise of

17

new religious movements; and

8. The phenomenally rapid growth of T.V. coverage of the news.

The list could, of course, go on, but our point is made. The sixties were times of rapid social change and significant social turmoil. As Carroll has said, those "who lived through that decade may....find it difficult to comprehend the number and variety of significant changes and upheavals that occured."27 Surely, religion and religious commitment were not left untouched by these events. If the 1960's were the years in which the society struck-out in new and novel directions, the 1970's were the years in which much of the latent distrust of basic institutions became manifest. Again, several events and dramas are easily identifiable as contributing to the distrust and disillusionment of Americans. Consider just four:

1. The killing of student protestors at Kent State and Jackson State universities;

2. The "strategic withdrawal" of American combat forces from Viet Nam;

3. The Mid-East oil embargo and its attendant influence on all facets of American life; and

4. The Watergate scandal, and the first American President to resign from that office.

These four events are alone sufficient to shake the confidence of Americans in their government and political parties. But if the many national studies are correct, the distrust and cynicism have spilled over to all major social institutions-- corporations, schools, churches, medicine, the press, and marriage. Americans, it seems, have turned more and more toward a sort of lonely individualism-- what David Riesman has called "privatization."28

As T. George Harris has pointed out about Americans, "while giving up faith in institutions, studies show, they continue to demand more and more of themselves in terms of both achievement and that new obsession with self-fulfillment." An important question is the extent to which the human psyche can continue to be estranged from basic support institutions while expecting greater success and higher self-fulfillment.29 It seems to us that men and women are clearly social creatures, and to turn from their social institutions to a dependency on purely individual achievement places and extremely heavy price on their already precarious existence. As Harris so poignantly put it, the notion of privatization "exposes the private man or woman to more of a burden than one soul can stand without wobbling."30

Harris goes on to provide an insightful illustration of the near impossible demands placed on Americans by virtue of this trend toward privatization:31

> In marriage, for instance, a woman now expects herself to be an accomplished bedmate, an intellectual equal, a wise and loving mother, perhaps a fellow jogger and tennis partner and smart tourist, one who continues to grow, a community organizer and co-host, often a co-professional, and almost always a fellow breadwinner. We expect similar miracles from ourselves at work; aside from earning the highest pay ever known, we expect to be sensitive to co-workers, enlarge our education, make a social contribution, and do very little damage to the environment. The average education of the active worker is now that of a college freshman after Christmas, and still going up.

Of course, critical evaluators of the American social scene have decried these developments as symptomatic of a "new narcissism" or the advent of the "me decade." But again, as Harris points out, there is "less selfishness than loneliness in the American psyche today, along with the feeling of being called upon to do heroic things without warm support from good old reliables like the Democratic party, the Catholic Church, or Good Mother Company."32

19

What are the implications of this for America and Americans in the 1980's? Will Herberg has suggested that in our society a paramount question is:33

> "What am I?" . . .is perhaps the most immediate [question] that a man can ask himself in the course of his social life. Everyone finds himself in a social context which he shares with many others, but within this social context, how shall he locate himself? Unless he can so locate himself, he cannot tell himself, and others will not be able to know, who and what he is; . . .To live, he must "belong"; to "belong," he must be able to locate himself in the larger social whole to identify himself to himself and to others.

Of course we are concerned, in these pages, with religion and religious commitment. We must ask, therefore, what is the importance of Herberg's analysis for our discussion. We will let Herberg answer this question for us:34

> And although this process of self-identification and social location is not in itself intrinsically religious, the mere fact that in order to be "something" one must be a Protestant, Catholic, or a Jew means that one begins to think of oneself as religiously identified and affiliated.

And here is the rub, during the period 1965-75, the majority of mainline Protestant churches lost membership, to wit: United Presbyterian, down 12.2%; United Methodist, down 10.1%; United Church of Christ, down 12.2%; Presbyterian U.S., down 7.6%; Lutheran Church in America, down 5.0%; and Episcopal, down 16.7%. Roman Catholics continued to grow, but at a highly attenuated rate (only 8.7% during 1965-1975 as compared with 38.5% during 1955-1965). Those churches that did experience growth were, by and large, the more fundamentalist or conservative organizations (Church of the Nazarene, Assemblies of God, Seventh-Day Adventist, and Southern Baptist).35 Where have all of these church members gone?

On first blush one might be tempted to say the answer is obvious. Didn't we just say that the mainliners have declined and the conservatives have grown? Isn't it clear that the church members have gone to the Church of the Nazarene, the Assemblies of God, and other similar churches. Not really. The losses of the mainliners are too large for the growth in the smaller, more conservative church groups to accomodate them, even with phenomenal growth. It might be argued that the Southern Baptists are large, a fact that cannot be denied. But of the various conservative churches, Southern Baptists had the smallest growth rate for the period of time under consideration. Again, we ask, where have all of the members gone? .

The options, it seems, are three. First, the losses may have been absolute. That is, these ex-members may have abandoned religion completely, no longer believing or practicing any form of religion. Second, the lost members may remain identified with religion, albeit only on an irregular basis, going to a Baptist church one Sunday, and a Methodist or Presbyterian church four or five worship days later. These persons have not deserted their religion; they may very well be part of those people identified by Glenn Vernon as the "religious nones." Finally, it may be that some of the losses of the mainliners have also been losses to the conservative churches, but not to religion altogether. It is entirely within the realm of possibility that thousands upon thousands of these "lost sheep" have been "found" by what Hadden and Swann have called the "Prime Time Preachers" of the Electronic Church.36

The extent to which the Mass Media Ministers have attracted the American viewing public is not totally clear. There is a large gap between the claims of audience size made by the T.V. preachers, and the results of viewer monitoring by the Arbitron and Nielson rating services. For example, Ben Armstrong, in his book entitled The Electric Church, says that close to 130 million people tune in religious radio and television programs on any given Sunday.37 Armstrong is himself a strong advocate of the evangelical message. Apparently, however, even the secular press has been so impressed by the religious broadcasters and their claims about audience size that it too has claimed huge audiences for the Mass Media Ministers. In fact, the Wall Street Journal stated that just three of the T.V. preachers-- Oral Roberts, Pat Robertson, and Jerry Falwell-- have a weekly audience of 128 million viewers.38 Even Playboy magazine has attributed exceptionally large audiences to the T.V. preachers. Not to be outdone, Rex Humbard once claimed as many as 100 million viewers for his program alone!39

While the T.V. preachers and the secular press have been claiming large audiences for Christian television, Arbitron has estimated the total viewership for syndicated Christian television programs to be approximately 21.5 million.40 For the month of February, 1980, Arbitron data indicated that evangelist Jimmy Swaggart had an audience size of 1,986,000.41 Three years later, Swaggart's magazine, The Evangelist, claimed to have the "number one television audience" according to Arbitron's rating for July, 1983.42 According to the Swaggart magazine, "In the past four years the television audience has almost doubled. Nearly 3,000,000 people each week tune in over 250 stations in more than 180 television markets to watch Jimmy Swaggart." However, Jerry Falwell's "Old Time Gospel Hour" also claims to be the "nations largest syndicated religious program," broadcast on "392 television and nearly 600 radio stations."43 Given the contradictory claims, it is difficult to estimate viewership of religious programming with any reliability.

Even Arbitron, which has accurate data, has incomplete data because of sparse coverage of the more than 4,000 cable systems in America. We find this a significant hole in the available data. In 1983, we surveyed a 20 percent random sample of cable subscribers in a city of approximately 50,000. While the cable system carried Jim Bakker's PTL Network, that particular channel was not included on the survey questionnaire mailed to the sample of cable subscribers. Interestingly, however, as the questionnaires began to be returned, we noticed that 26 percent of those who responded had actually taken the time to write-in that they watched PTL! Furthermore, a very large percentage of people we ask about the T.V. preachers say they have watched them at least once. Most of the people with whom we speak also express negative opinions about the television preachers-- a substantial portion, however, express positive

22

feelings.

How many folks watch religious television? We don't know, but we suspect that the number is substantially less than the T.V. preachers and the secular press have claimed. We would also want to suggest that the audience is somewhat larger than Arbitron credits to Christian television. Whatever the actual count, the number is large enough to serve to alert us to the fact that we are talking about a significant social phenomenon in American society.

BAITING THE HOOK: ON GETTING AND KEEPING MASS MEDIA MEMBERS

25

BAITING THE HOOK: ON GETTING AND KEEPING MASS MEDIA MEMBERS

INTRODUCTION

When Jesus came into the coasts of Cesarea
Philippi, he asked his disciples, saying, Whom
do men say that I, the Son of man, am? And they
said, Some say that thou art John the Baptist;
some, Elias; and others, Jeremias, or one of the
prophets. He saith unto them, But whom say ye
that I am? And Simon Peter answered and said,
Thou are the Christ, the Son of the living God.
And Jesus answered and said unto him, Blessed art
thou, Simon Bar-jona: for flesh and blood hath
not revealed it unto thee, but my Father which
is in heaven. And I say also unto thee, That
thou art Peter, and upon this rock I will build
my church; and the gates of hell shall not prevail
against it.

Matthew 16:13-19

As we have already seen, the period of time from
1965 to 1975 was not "good news" as regards membership
in the mainline, Protestant churches in America. Almost

27

all of the "mainliners" experienced significant drops in membership, while the smaller, more conservative groups were having important growth in their membership. Even if the growth among the conservative religions was sufficient to offset the losses of the mainliners (an outcome we consider highly unlikely), a quick check with the U.S. Bureau of the Census would show that relative to population growth, the mainliners suffered rather large losses. This assumes, of course, that the mainline churches should be expected to show some growth; growth that paralleled, or was consistent with, increases in the general population. However, during 1965-1975, the mainliners began to experience absolute membership losses, even as the U.S. population continued to grow. As Carroll, Johnson, and Marty suggest:1

> Protestants grew more rapidly than the total population through the Post World War II period, down to 1955. During the 1955-1965 decade, Protestant growth generally paralleled that of the population. From 1965 to 1970, Protestants continued to grow, but at a rate slightly less than the total population; and from 1970 to 1973 the total number of Protestants showed a very slight loss (less than 1 percent).

Although Carroll, Johnson, and Marty are correct in their analysis, there are, nevertheless, important points that need to be made in order to supplement their analysis. First, they included among the Protestant churches "some bodies which, strictly speaking, are non-Protestant, such as Latter Day Saints (Mormons) and Jehovah's Witnesses." Correcting for these groups by removing them as part of traditional Protestant bodies, would show that mainline Protestant churches have lost more than one percent. There is a second factor to consider. Of the mainline Protestant denominations, Southern Baptists are clearly one of the most conservative (if not the most conservative), and they continued to show growth during the 1965-1975 period. If we were to remove the Southern Baptists and look only at the moderate to liberal groups (Lutheran, Presbyterian, Episcopalian, Church of Christ, Congregationalist, and Methodist), the losses of the moderate to liberal Protestant churches would be large indeed. We would be relatively safe in suggesting that during the 1965-1975 decade, moderate to liberal Protestant churches lost in the neighborhood of at least two and one-half million members. However, we are discussing this about ten years after 1975, and many events have happened in our society since that time. Consider the following:

1. Jimmy Carter, an avowed "born again" Christian, is elected President of the U.S. in 1976;

2. With the blessings of the Ayatollah Khoemni,Americans are held as hostages in Iran;

3. The Reverend Jerry Falwell emerges as a spokesman for the New Christian Right. He forms the "Moral Majority" in 1979;

4. Ronald Reagan is elected President of the U.S. in 1980;

5. President Reagan declares 1983 to be "The Year of the Bible";

6. There is an attempted assassination of the Pope;

7. U.S. Marines are deployed as "peacekeepers" in Beriut, and 241 of them die as a result of a terrorist bombing;

8. The Island of Grenada is invaded by forces of the United States;

9. The United States has the highest unemployment rate in our society since the great depression; and

10. President Reagan establishes diplomatic relations with the Vatican; and

11. Although it did not get the required two-thirds majority, President Reagan's Oral School Prayer Amendment did have more U.S. Senators vote for it than voted against it.

Of course, our list could go on. We mention these events in order to point-out that social change is an on-going process and its effects make long-term forecasting about society difficult. It is against this backdrop that we will mention some forecasts about religion made by the famous pollster, Dr. George Gallup.

In 1976, George Gallup conducted one of his many surveys and, based on the results, suggested that 1976 was a turning point in church membership in America. According to Gallup, "our 1976 surveys showed church membership to be on the upswing during the year with about 7 in 10 describing themselves as church members."2 In 1977, membership statistics showed no change, and because membership decline did not reappear, Dr. Gallup's forecast for future membership in religious bodies was a positive one. Keeping in mind that much has happened in the interim between Dr. Gallup's forecast and the present time, we can inquire as to whether he was generally correct in his judgment. In general, we can say that Gallup was correct because membership decline does seem to have leveled-off. However, these are general, nationwide trends, and particular areas, or particular religions, may move counter to them. The State of Kentucky is one such example. The available information indicates that between 1970 and 1980, membership losses in mainline, traditional Protestant churches has ranged from 11 to 21 percent in Kentucky. What we have then, is the proverbial "mixed-bag" of data which may be due, in part, to the quality of information kept by religious bodies.

In view of recent trends, many people have trumpeted the arrival of a new religious revival in America. It appears that support for a religious revival in America is coming from the highest echelons of government in this country. We would want to suggest that the transition from Jimmy Carter to Ronald Reagan in the White House saw no decline in the enthusiam of the President for religion. In fact, the 1980 Presidential campaign is notable for the involvement of the New Christian Right in the political affairs of this nation at an unprecendented level. In many ways, the television became the "bully pulpit" of the New Christian Right. Through the programming of of Jerry Falwell, Pat Robertson, Jim Bakker, Jimmy Swaggart, Rex Humbard, Oral Roberts, and other T.V. preachers, it continues to be so into the present time.

If there is a new religious revival in America today, there is, in addition, a new participant in that movement that the traditional, mainline churches must take into account. They must share the "fruits" of the revival with the recently emerged "Electronic Church," headed by those Hadden and Swann have called the "Prime Time Preachers."3

We have discussed membership losses in the mainline, Protestant churches. We mentioned two kinds of membership losses: (1) absolute losses, and (2) relative losses as a result of a failure to keep pace with general population growth. When the absolute and relative losses are coupled together, decline in church membership takes on a new dimension of importance. We asked this question before, and here, early in this Chapter, we ask it again: "Where have all of the parishioners (members) gone?" One answer, for some of these lost parishioners, is that they have gone to the "Electronic Church." We do not want to suggest that all, or even the majority of them, have gone to the Mass Media Ministers. We do, however, want to suggest that many probably have, and from the point-of-view of the "mainliners," the number is not insignificant.

Will Herberg has suggested that a sense of social location is essential in answering the question "What am I?"4 Herberg also pointed-out that in America, the ability to locate oneself religiously has been an important component of an answer to that question. Being Protestant, Catholic, or Jewish has been, in general, an important part of one's personal identity. Within the Protestant identity, being Southern Baptist as opposed to American Baptist, Methodist, Episcopalian, Presbyterian, and so on, has been of particular significance for our notions of who and what we are as Americans. But as David Reisman has pointed-out, and T. George Harriss has emphasized, Americans have turned away from institutional involvement and turned inward through the process of "privatization."5 We have done so, not because we no longer need or require social anchoring, but out of a distrust and cynicism for our basic social, political, and religious organizations; a distrust that has been nurtured into a third decade by mismanagement and scandal by those very institutions. While the need for social location remains present in the American psyche, an unwillingness to place trust in basic institutions has created a void of loneliness in the American population. We believe that it is into this void that the Electronic Church and the Mass Media Ministers are stepping as we move into the decade of the 80's, and beyond.

CREATING AND MAINTAINING MASS MEDIA MEMBERS

And Jesus came and spake unto them, saying,
All power is given unto me in heaven and in
earth.
Go ye therefore, and teach all nations,
baptizing them in the name of the Father, and
of the Son, and of the Holy Ghost: Teaching them
to observe all things whatsoever I have commanded
you: and, lo, I am with you alway, even unto the
end of the world. Amen.

Matthew 28:18-20

An important question facing sociologists, anthropologists, psychologists, and other watchers of religion in America is how the television preachers get, and hold, the viewers they have. There are, of course, many factors involved in attracting viewers and holding them as members. It may be that some people who are concerned about religious television will be offended by our using the label "members" to characterize those people who watch, regularly and frequently, Christian television. However, whether they are called "PTL Club Partners," "Faith Partners," "members of the "700 Club," the "Eagle Club," or something else, many of these viewers do consider themselves to be members in the same sense that others are counted as members of a local congregation. We make no apologies for calling these people "members."

After just a few hours of watching Pat Robertson's "700 Club," Jim Bakker's "PTL Club'" Jimmy Swaggart's Crusades, or other religious television, the viewer comes away with the general impression that the Prime Time Preachers broadcast with quality television programming. The formating, the sets, the camera work, and the music all point to a high level of professionalism in the origination and delivery of the religious message. That the message may not always be exclusively religious has been alleged and argued for the past several years.5 It is a subject we will deal with later in this book. For now, however, our attention is focused on how television ministers create and maintain "mass media members."

Given the formating, the sets, and so forth, it seems obvious to us that the television ministers have done their homework. In an address given on Jim Bakker's PTL Club, the Rev. Rex Humbard said, "In this business of the television ministry, we have to have the best technicians, the best singers, the best facilities, and the timing has to be perfect." After several hundred hours of watching the Electronic Church, we are convinced that the other television preachers have paid close attention to the statement by the Rev. Humbard. He is, of course, one of the Deans of the television ministry. In the same address on Bakker's PTL Club, Humbard said that when he first saw a television program some thirty years ago, he knew that this medium would be the way to reach millions with the message of Christ. Today, the Mass Media Ministers claim to be reaching millions of mass media members via television.

To enumerate the general way in which they attract people and hold the support of people, we will list some of the methods they use to accomplish this. We will discuss each of these methods. Judging from the amount of money they are able to raise, and the size of the viewing audience they claim, it seems clear that their game plan is working.

Some of the things which seem most useful in the ability of television preachers to get and hold members are these:

> 1. They often have big-name, celebrity guests who testify to being "born again" Christians, and who give support to the television ministry;
>
> 2. They involve the participants in a cause greater than themselves;

3. They present a concept of a God who is ready to come into the individual believer's life in a very personal way;

4. They stress the internalization of religious commitment and the social aspects of that commitment;

5. They quite often, directly or indirectly, attack the mainline, organized churches;

6. They stress the healing ministry via television;

7. They stress the idea, that, as a person gives to God's work on the television ministry, God gives back to that person a hundred times over;

8. They have a very efficient system of follow-up on their respondents which could not be done without the use of computer technology;

9. In keeping with Will Herberg's point concerning religious membership as providing social location important to a sense of personal identity, the Electronic Church makes provision for such social anchoring.

As indicated earlier, we will discuss, in a general way, how the Mass Media Ministers employ each of the above points to create and maintain their mass media members.

The Provision for a Sense of Belonging

Now I beseech you, brethren, by the name of our Lord Jesus Christ, that ye all speak the same thing, and that there be no divisions among you; but that ye be perfectly joined together in the same mind and in the same judgement.

I Corinthians 1:10

On the "700 Club," Ben Kinchlow gave a talk on the "born again" experience, in which he sketched what he saw as the Biblical and theological basis for the validity of that experience. He described the various things which will happen to a person who is "born again"; events which included forgiveness, acceptance by God and the "family" of God, a sense of direction in the person's life, and finally, according to Kinchlow, the person will "have a feeling of belonging." He went on to say "you do not have to be afraid or ashamed of facing the world. You know that God is walking with you through the problems you may face in your life situation."

The television preachers are of one mind on this subject, although they present the concept in different ways. To a person, the Prime Time Preachers say that one of the benefits of being "born again" is to gain a sense of personal worth and belonging to the larger family of believers. Theologically speaking, the position of the T.V. preachers is not very different from what the church universal has believed and taught. The shift in emphasis is not on the content of the Gospel message. Mainline churches such as the United Methodists, the Baptists, and others, have long preached a message of personal redemption and a personal relationship with God; a message that is as old as the earliest records of the Christian church. In the Epistle to the Romans by St. Paul, we find "The Spirit itself bears witness with our spirit, that we are the children of God (Romans 8:16)." There are many statements throughout the New Testament and 2,000 years of the history of the Christian church which bear witness to this concept.

As mentioned earlier in this chapter, the sociologist Will Herberg has pointed out that a sense of religious belonging has been important to Americans. Americans are, most social scientists would agree, among the most religious people on earth. Given these ideas, the question again arises, why have people left the mainline churches, and why have many of them turned to the television ministry? As we have said earlier, there have been many disruptive events in American society over the past three decades. One result has been that many Americans have become distrustful of the

35

established institutions. The T.V. ministry seems to be providing an outlet for people, who in spite of their distrust of old, familiar institutions, still need to have a sense of belonging. A cursory glance at the message of the T.V. preachers demonstrates that they are providing that sense of religious belonging for a significant number of Americans.

If the message the T.V. preachers proclaim is not substantially different from the historical Christian tradition, wherein lies their success? We will, in another chapter, discuss the way in which the T.V. evangelists use the medium as their message. For now, we can confidently state that the message is not the only vehicle for their success. The methods the Mass Media Ministers use provide an understanding of their success, a large measure of which comes from their ability to convey a sense of belonging to many people.

When a person joins the "PTL Club," the "700 Club," or any of the other ways of participating in the T.V. ministry, then one belongs. The person who joins and commits him or herself to prayer and giving becomes part of a larger group that is engaged in the same activities. The implications for an extension of the "self," and the connections of that "self" with the larger world are, from the point of view of social psychology, significant. Judging by the number of persons who call on the toll-free numbers as a means of joining the T.V. ministry, it seems obvious that they want to belong. They are also getting, not just personal religion, but a sense of the social self; a social self that is also part of their personal relationship as a born again believer. Indeed, it is presented by the T.V. ministers as flowing from that relationship. The social sciences have demonstrated that people need a sense of identity, an identity which can only be established in the presence of other humans. It is clear from the standpoint of the religious self, and the social self, that we humans can feel that we belong to a meaningful group. It is also clear, from the findings of social psychology, that when humans feel that they belong, they will act on that sense of belonging. This is one more element of human conduct which is important to the methods of the Mass Media Ministers.

The Greater Cause

Know ye not that they which run in a race run
all, but one receiveth the prize? So run, that
ye may obtain. And every man that striveth for
the mastery is temperate in all things. Now
they do it to obtain a corruptible crown; but we
an incorruptible.I therefore so run, not as
uncertainly; so fight I, not as one that beateth
the air: But I keep under my body, and bring it
into subjection: lest that by any means, when I
have preached to others, I myself should be a
castaway.

I Corinthians 9:24-27

        When   a   person   chooses   to   become   an   active
supporter   of   the   T.V.   ministry, that person is told
that   he   or   she has become part of a great cause. The
cause   is no less than the salvation of people all over
the   world.   The   cause   is   no   less   than   to reshape
societies,   in   this   country   and abroad, to fit God's
plan   to   the   world. Once again, this concept is not a
new   one   in   the   history   of   Christianity.   But   the
television preachers are able to bring many millions of
people,   and   thus   many millions of dollars, into this
proclaimed   cause. The cause they proclaim is the great
commission   of   Jesus: "Go   ye therefore and teach all
nations,   baptizing them in the name of the Father, and
of   the   Son,   and   of the Holy Ghost (Mt. 28:19)." The
cause   they   proclaim also includes changing the world.
This   cause,   according to the T.V. preachers, includes
changing   the   society   in   which the new member lives.
According to the Mass Media Ministers, when one becomes
a   giving member of their particular T.V. ministry, one
also   becomes   a full-fledged participant in God's plan
to make a better world. The viewer is invited to belong
to   an   organization which is carrying out this plan of
God.

        It   is   important   to   recognize   that   the   plan
includes   more   than the saving of individual souls. It
includes   what   has has been referred to as the "social
gospel," which includes support for feeding the hungry,

building schools, training people in the ministry, changing laws to make them more in line with the gospel, and many other things.

The invitation to the prospective T.V. church member to become active in changing society is not a side-show; it is part of the "main event!" When the issues are cast in the light of being at the foundation of the religious in American society, and the ultimate concern of the true believer in Christianity (as defined by the T.V. preachers), the new and prospective members are placed in the position of really having only two choices. Those choices are to join the great movement of religious revival as demonstrated on T.V., or to abandon their personal faith as well as their faith in their country.

When one looks at the history of the world, and more specifically, at the history of Western Civilization, it is clear that large numbers of people will join, and have joined, what they perceive to be "great causes." The Crusades of the Middle Ages attracted thousands of people to a "great cause." The cause was to free the Holy Land from the infidels. The Reformation was a great cause. The cause was to throw off the perceived yolk of the the Roman church on society, and on the individual. Many millions of people joined these causes. The day after the Japanese bombed Pearl Harbor thousands of men lined up in front of military recruiting offices to join the armed forces of the United States. The cause was defense of the country. Martin Luther King, Jr., was able to muster hundreds of thousands of people in the cause of civil rights. These examples, and others, make it clear that people will make their presence known for a cause in which they believe. This is no less true for the religious cause of reshaping, saving, and bringing America back to God's plan for this country. People will also vote their "lives, their fortune, and their sacred honor" in a cause which is in opposition to the powers that be. The turmoil of the Vietnam Era makes this obvious.

People who join the television ministry are told by the T.V. preachers that they are joining a great cause. They are told that their cause is no less than the plan of God for themselves, and for their country. Since the United States is the "light to the nations," then the cause is all humanity. The cause is global!

38

Pat Robertson, president of Christian Broadcasting Network (CBN), is calling 1984 the year of "America at the Crossroads," and the Rev. Jerry Falwell claims that 1984 is "The Year of Destiny." These television preachers are saying that there is a "great cause" to join. The television preachers stress that now is a wonderful opportunity to join this "great cause" of saving religious freedom, and the freedom of America as well. In view of history, it should be no surprise that people are joining in this great cause; and they are joining in with their financial support, as well.

The Internalization of Religious Commitment

I therefore, the prisoner of the Lord, beseech you that ye walk worthy of the vocation wherewith ye are called, With all lowliness and meekness, with longsuffering, forbearing one another in love; Endeavouring to keep the unity of the Spirit in the bond of peace. There is one body, and one spirit, even as ye are called in one hope of your calling; One Lord, one faith, one baptism, One God and Father of all, who is above all, and through all, and in you all.

Ephesians 4:1-6

Prime Time television preachers hammer away at an old Biblical tradition. The tradition we have in mind is that commitment to God is a matter of the "heart"; that is, it is a matter of internalizing the components of religious commitment. In this concept of religious commitment it is not enough to "go through the motions" of religious commitment. As we have mentioned in the first chapter, sociology has long been interested in measuring religious commitment, but has, by and large, missed this important component of it.

It is our position that many people who have not been able to internalize religious commitment in the traditional modes have turned to the cathode church.

Further, we believe, that many of those whom Vernon called the religious "nones" utilize television church to aid them in the internalization of their religious beliefs and values. In doing so they get a great deal of positive reinforcement from the T.V. preachers to help them in their quest. Once again, we feel that it is important to reemphasize that the message the television preachers proclaim is strictly Biblical. They do not depart from anything that the mainline churches have historically taught.

Martin Luther taught at the beginning of the Protestant Reformation in Germany that the individual believer had direct access to God. Thus, one did not need the services of a priest or an organized church, to gain access, in prayer and life, to God. This has been called the "Protestant principle." That is, one can talk directly to God without benefit of a priest. Another term which has been used in this connection is the "Priesthood of all believers." Since Luther based his belief on the Gospel, the teachings/letters of St. Paul, and a doctor of the church, St. Augustine, it is obvious that these ideas were old in the church even in Luther's time.

The Methodist Revival in England in the 1700's also stressed the internalization of religious commitment. John Wesley had a religious experience at Aldresgate Street in London, England. He said, his "heart was strangely warmed. I knew that Christ had died for me." Later, he wrote that he knew that he was a new person. From this religious experience of John Wesley, over a period of time, the United Methodist Church has come into existence.

These two examples serve to show, out of the many examples which could be given, that the concept of God reaching into the personality of the believer is not new. The Bible is replete with stories such as these. Whatever interpretation one may place on these experiences, one thing is sure, they were real for the persons involved. Another thing is sure, out of these experiences came movements which changed societies.

The T.V. preachers make it plain that they believe that the "born again" experience is, first and foremost, an internalization of religious commitment. They say with one voice that God comes into the believer's life and experience in a very personal way.

40

It is not just a ritual experience! In one of his sermons, the Reverend Jerry Falwell said, "You can die and go to hell if you are religious or moral. You cannot be Christian unless you have been born again." He went on to say that you are not a Christian simply because you have been baptized in the church in which you were raised.

In stressing the internalization of religious commitment, the television preachers are generally in the mainstream of Christian theology. The question again arises, therefore, "What do they have that others do not?" As this chapter, and this book developes, we hope to give some viewpoints on this vexing question. To set the background for an answer to this question we believe that while the overt message of the television preachers is at the heart of their presentation, the methods they use in presenting it represent the life force that pumps that heart.

The Attack on the Mainline Churches

He that hath an ear, let him hear what the
Spirit saith unto the churches. And unto the
angel of the church of the Laodiceans write;
These things saith the Amen, the faithful and
true witness, the beginning of the creation of
God; I know thy works, that thou are neither
cold nor hot, I will spue thee out of my mouth.

Revelation 3:13-16

It seems to us that if the Mass Media Ministers are to keep their mass media members, they must present themselves as a viable, and perhaps desirable, alternative to the mainline churches. One way of accomplishing this is to cast doubt on the appropriateness of the message of the mainliners. In a word, attack the mainliners from a biblical base.

That the T.V. preachers have attacked, and continue to attack the mainline churches can be verified by simply watching the cathode church. The statements below are only a few of the negative

41

comments we have heard about the mainline churches and their ministers, on the television ministry. In these attacks on the mainline churches, the television preachers often seem to come from an attitude of the ancient prophets of Israel. One can also detect a spirit such as is found in the book of Revelation in the New Testament. In that book, angels are represented as speaking to the Christian churches. Because some of these churches have been apostate, the angel says that God wants no part of them. At one point, an angel says to an established church, "I will spew thee out of my mouth (Rev.3)." There are times when the television preachers say this, and similar things about the mainline churches. An idea the television preachers often try to convey is that the mainline churches, and their organized ministry, have missed the gospel message. Therefore, they are not ministering to the flock.

In a crusade in Birmingham, Alabama, the Reverend Jimmy Swaggart made a most dramatic attack. He said to that audience, "Don't let any church tell you that their teaching is equal to the Bible." In a sermon delivered during his Albuquerque crusade, to a packed stadium, Swaggart said, "chuches who do not preach the true Word of God should have the name church ripped off their doors."(We wonder if only Jimmy Swaggart knows the "true" Word of God.) Swaggart said these things as he referred to a poll of preachers which was conducted several years ago. In that poll, a large sample of ordained ministers were asked certain questions concerning their religious beliefs. The questions had to do with what nearly all mainline Protestant churches state as a belief. The questions were about belief in the Bible as the Word of God, Heaven, Hell, and so forth. One could sum up the questons in the Apostles Creed. A fairly large percentage of the preachers responding to the survey stated that they did not believe these things, or were undecided. Reverend Swaggart (looking into the T.V. camera) said, "you preachers who have this unbelief are servants of the Devil." He then said to the audience, "if you are going to a church where the preacher is this way, you should get out." When Swaggart made these statements, the audience stood and gave him an ovation, roaring their approval. He obviously struck a responsive chord in most of the people who were there.

The Reverend James Robison, in a sermon delivered

on CBN was equally critical of the mainline churches. The subject of his sermon was the apostacy of the church. He said "the people in the church are filled with demons. I will never again preach to make a church look good with new members." The total content of the sermon was the thesis that one needs to be born again, and that a person does not have to go to church to be born again and follow Christ. Just before he gave the call for members of the audience to come and be "born again," he made another statement about the churches. He said, "you people out there do not need to hear the lies in the church. You need the truth and the truth will set you free."

It is not too unusual to see programs on the Christian networks in which some person makes a statement about failing to find faith in the regular (mainline) church. On a PTL Club Show, a lady from South Dakota told how the pastor in her church had told her not to watch television church. She did, however, and was saved. She stated that she felt that the organized churches were against the television ministry. The Reverend Robison said in a sermon that his crusades had been boycotted by the mainline churches in some cities where he had preached.

Of all of the T.V. evangelists, Jimmy Lee Swaggart has launched the most vocal, and the most vicious attacks on the mainline churches in general, and on specific personages, in particular. Although we do not agree with Newsweek that Swaggart is "the acknowledged king of the electronic church," we do recognize his voice to be one of the most powerful among the media ministers.6 In October of 1983, Swaggart displayed gruesome photos taken at Auschwitz and other Nazi death camps, "seeming to suggest that the extermination of 6 million Jews was the result of their failure to believe in Jesus Christ."7 Swaggart has also suggested that Mother Teresa of Calcutta will go to hell unless she is "born again." The holocaust broadcast resulted in television station WLVI in Boston, cancelling Swaggart's show. During his Birmingham crusade, Swaggart attacked the doctrine of predestination, suggesting that churches that teach such a doctrine have lead, and are leading, "millions" to hell. Swaggart has been so persistent in criticizing Roman Catholicism that WANX, a station owned by CBN, dropped his broadcasts. Although Swaggart steadfastly claims that he loves Catholics and Jews, his tirades

43

against both continue unabated.

Why do many respond, in an approving way, to these attacks on the mainline churches? It is obvious, when one observes the people responding, that this attack reaches many people where they think. For some time there has been a general unhappiness with the mainline churches. This was evidenced by the previously mentioned decline in church membership. The entire number of church pews in the United States will not accommodate, at any given time, more than a small percentage of the population. This means that if any great number of people in this country were to decide to go to church, they could not. The churches simply could not hold them!

It seems reasonable then, that there are many people in this society who are not involved in the established churches. This recalls Glenn Vernon's concept of the religious "nones." All of this serves to reinforce our belief that large numbers of people are being reached by the television preachers. The majority of the "pews" of the television preachers are the recliners, the easy chairs, the couches, and the beds of an ordinary American house. These have become the cathedrals of the television church. With these things in mind, it is not difficult to understand why many people applaud the attacks on the mainline churches. They seem to have a perception of a bureaucratic church which does not minister to people in the way that the television ministry does.8

There is one last area where the television preachers can level an attack on the organized, mainline churches. Once again though, this seeming advantage the television ministry has is related to the electronic technology they have learned to use so well. The area we speak of is that very large percentage of the population that is home-bound, or living in care facilities of various sorts. We speak here of the elderly and disabled people in this country. Since it is beyond the ability of these people to get out and go to regular worship services, they are dependent on two main sources of religious outreach. One is the visit(s) of their local pastor; the other is the church on television. The varied duties of the ordinary church minister hardly allow him or her to spend as much time with his home-fast, bed-fast church members as his church members can spend with the television church.

Here seems to be an area of real need which the
television ministry meets. There are other places which
the television ministry has opened to communication, and
we will discuss them in a later chapter.

Whether or not these attacks on the mainline churches
are justified, one thing is clear. Such attacks often
strike a very responsive chord among those who view the
Mass Media Ministers. There are many people who, while
considering themselves to be religious, have no
connection with a mainline church. We are convinced that
many of them find an outlet for their religious
commitment on the T.V. ministry of the cathode church.
Another outlet is that of the healing ministry of the
T.V. church. We will now turn our attention to the ways
in which the television preachers stress this very old
tradition in Christianity. It clearly serves as a
vehicle through which mass media members can be created
and maintained.

The Healing Ministry

    And it came to pass the day after, that he
went into a city called Nain; and may of his
disciples went with him, and much people.
    Now when he came nigh to the gate of the city,
behold, there was a dead man carried out, the
only son of his mother, and she was a widow;
and much people of the city was with her. And
when the Lord saw her, he had compassion on her,
and said unto her, Weep not.
    And he came and touched the bier: an they that
bare him stood still. And he said, Young man, I
say unto thee, Arise. And he that was dead sat
up, and began to speak. And he delivered him to
his mother.

Luke 7:11-15

    On many occasions the television preachers make

use of the healing ministry, a ministry that has a background reaching back to the time of Jesus' ministry. The New Testament makes much of the tradition that Jesus healed people by his power in the Spirit, through the laying on of hands and other physical manifestations of the power of the Spirit of God. Moreover, the text of the New Testament makes it plain that the early church believed in the power of healing. There is hardly a book in the entire New Testament which does not mention the power of healing. In a New Testament book which the great reformer, Martin Luther, did not think much of, there is a reference to healing. That book is the Epistle of James. Martin Luther called it an epistle of straw, suggesting that it should be thrown into Eliba River because it makes little use of the name of Jesus. But the television preachers often quote James in connection with their healing ministry. They quote the verses which say "Is any sick among you? Let him call for the elders of the church; and let them pray over him, annointing him with oil in the name of the Lord. And the prayer of faith shall save the sick...(James 5:14-15)." The healing ministry on television is an old tradition in the Christian faith. It is, therefore, not surprising that this aspect of television religion is very effective.

In stressing the healing ministry, television preachers once again strike a responsive chord which gets and holds members of the total television ministry. They pray for the healing of people on television and claim responses from people who have been healed as a result of prayer via television. On a typical one hour program, these responses come in by the scores. To give examples: On the "700 Club," Pat Robertson and his Co-hosts regularly pray for the healing Spirit of God to affect people all over the United States. The form of the praying is that the major participants (Pat and his Co-hosts) join hands and pray for people to be healed. After the prayers, the phones are ringing incessantly. Many calls are reported by the prayer counselors who man the phones. The reports typically include many people saying that they have "claimed" the healing message of Pat and/or the others, and they have been healed while praying along with the television preachers.

It is well known that Oral Roberts achieved fame as a healing minister. The healing he did on television for years has become a legend in the field of television ministry. He is now in the process of building a hospital where medical science will be combined with Christian faith healing. He recently announced that he was "restoring" the healing ministry to his television programs. Shortly after that, on the Oral Roberts Show, his son, Richard Roberts, conducted a healing service. Richard Roberts laid his hands on people who came down, and they were healed. He looked out on the congregation and saw a person pushing an empty wheel-chair down the aisle. Richard asked, "Where is the person who was in the wheel-chair?" The man pushing it said, "They no longer use the wheel-chair." The congregation burst into applause. Many more people then came to the altar to be healed.

On the "PTL Club" show, Jim Bakker often has guests who testify to miraculous healing via T.V. church. Jim Bakker seems to be stressing the healing ministry more and more on his show. However, Bakker is not alone in doing this. Jimmy Swaggart also prays for people to be healed on his television crusades, and many people attending those crusades come to the altar to be healed. On one recent broadcast, a man in the audience began "speaking in tongues" while Jimmy Swaggart was praying. After the first man had finished "speaking in tongues," a second man translated the message into English. The people came by the hundreds to be saved and healed. At one point those who came to the altar stretched out their hands for a little crippled girl who had been brought to the altar. Reverend Swaggart laid his hands on her. It was a very emotional finale.

Perhaps the most obvious "healing show" on regular Christian television is a show called "Derin's Coffee Shop," with Derin and Rita Carmack. On this particular show, telecast on Jim Bakker's PTL Network, Derin and Rita ask people to call-in and tell them of what they, or someone they know, need to be healed. In general, Derin asks the caller her or his name, age, marital status, and so forth. After they have obtained this information, Derin asks his "partners" to "link-up" in prayer, and he begins to pray for healing...... "Now Father-God, we just come against that spirit of....." After the prayer of healing, either Derin or Rita inquire if the caller has a copy of their "scripture cards," exorting those who do not have them to be sure and send for them. After Derin and Rita tell about dynamic healings they have witnessed or know of, they take another phone call. Perhaps this time they pray for healing cancer of the colon, telling the caller they "see a bright, warm light" wrapping around the diseased colon and healing it. Numbers of those who call "Derin's Coffee Shop" are weeping as they do so. After they are prayed for, they are given the opportunity to send for the Carmack "scripture cards" (only $2.00) or to get a copy of "Rita Babe's" new book (for a donation of twenty dollars, or more). Perhaps Derin and Rita Carmack are serving a positive function on Christian television. We have our own opinion, but leave that for the reader to decide.

Clearly, there are many people who believe they can be healed of various infirmities via the television ministry. For these people such a belief is not a joke. It is real! We should not find this so surprising. This belief has a long history. If one thinks that these people are expecting the impossible, then one should notice the waiting room in his or her doctor's office; rooms which are usually full. People are waiting there for their physicians to give them treatment for their illnesses. For many illnesses, however, medical science has no cure. For many people with terminal illnesses, medical science can offer no hope beyond making these people's last days relatively free of physical pain. We say again, it is not surprising that so many people turn to the television ministry for healing. And this is one more way that the television preachers get, and hold, members. There are some members who pray, and there are some members who pray, pay, and are healed.

The Social Aspects of Being "Born Again"

And when he had called the people unto
him with his disciples also, he said unto
them, Whosoever will come after me, let
him deny himself, and take up his cross, and
follow me. For whosoever will save his life
shall lose it; but whosoever shall lose his
life for my sake and the gospel's, the same
shall save it. For what shall it profit a
man, if he shall gain the whole world, and
lose his own soul?

48

Mark 8:34-36

When we watch the television preachers we become aware that salvation is not just individual but also social, according to their interpretation; an interpretation that is not without basis in Biblical literature. The eighth century prophets of of Israel were very concerned with the social spects of religious commitment. Although they presented many viewpoints and perspectives on the social implications of religious commitment, they spoke with one voice on the concept that the God of Israel expected certain things from the religiously committed believer. These things included, a sense of the Holiness of God, a commitment to justice and mercy for the poor and oppressed , and a sense of the overriding presence of God over the destiny of nations. The eighth century prophets proclaimed the ever-presence of God in the affairs of state.

When the television preachers speak of the social implications of religious commitment, they are on solid Biblical ground. In doing this they speak both to people who are uncommitted and to those who are highly committed, in a persuasive and clear manner. The message is this: If you are born again, if you are committed, if you are a member of the family of God, then, you must be interested in changing your society. You must work to bring it into conformity with the revealed will of God. It is not by chance that the revealed will of God can be learned on television. To quote several of the television preachers, "God can use you to perform his works."

According to the television preachers, the social implications of the gospel take many forms. They include missionary activity around the world, the television ministry itself in America, and in as many as 120 other countries. Within the missionary activity there are, in addition to preaching the gospel, hospitals, schools, clinics, food programs, self-help programs and many others. Clearly the television ministry has "many irons in the fire." In a later chapter we will trace the development of these various television ministries. In doing so we will attempt to show that, while the last three decades were not "good

49

news" for mainline churches, they were "very good news" for the television ministry.

There is another direction which the television preachers are taking regarding social change. It is a direction which has profound implications for all of the people who live in the United States of America. The direction taken will probably lead to a U.S. Supreme Court decision. The television preachers have publicly stated that they will, henceforth, assume an active role in the affairs of this nation. They list several areas of concern for themselves, for all born again Christians, and for all supporters of their television ministries. These include: a constitutional amendment to allow prayer in schools, a bill to deny abortion on demand, and a desire to limit the access of homosexuals to certain areas of public life. These avowed goals for American life have been expressed on the PTL Club, the 700 Club, by Jimmy Swaggart, Jerry Falwell, and the Moral Majority. These same goals have also been espoused by many of the rising stars on the television church.

In late February, 1984, the Reverend Jerry Falwell appeared in Louisville, Kentucky, as the leader of the Moral Majority. He was in Louisville as part of a drive by Moral Majority to register two and one-half million voters sympathetic to the platform of that organization. During his Louisville stop, Falwell described 1984 as a year of destiny for conservatives. According to Falwell, "It's do or die for us."

What issues does Moral Majority consider critical in the political arena? Among others, the vital interests are voluntary prayer in school, a human life amendment to drastically curtail abortion on demand, pornography, and the use of drugs. In addition, Falwell said, "I can't imagine that, as individuals, any of our people would be interested in anyone other than Ronald Reagan," for president. Falwell insists that the issues of concern to the Moral Majority "are moral issues and were long before they become political." In suggesting that the New Religious Right needs to become involved in the political affairs of this nation, the Reverend Falwell stated that "conservative Christians and Jews have lost by default in the last 50 years. We have allowed somebody to tell us that religion and politics don't mix." He is putting America on notice that there is a new recipe-- one that calls for mixing many conservative Christians and Jews, with politics, and stiring well.

The people who are involved in the television ministry are an important segment of American society. It is true that evangelical, fundamentalist, and pentecostal people have been taken lightly in our society; they have often been the object of ridicule and scorn. However, we believe that the people who watch and contribute to the television ministry-- the mass media members-- are a significant factor in any understanding of the social forces present in American society today.

The goals of the T.V. ministers include social change; social change via governmental decrees. This is not new in American society. What the television preachers propose to their members is entirely within the framework of constitutional law. It is clear, however, they they have become yet another force to reckon with in American society. On the night that President Ronald Reagan announced his candidacy for President of the United States, the 700 Club was ending a fund raising drive. On that night, the 700 Club announced that the fund raising drive had raised over 5.2 million dollars a month from new members of the television church. Pat Robertson gave an opinion of President Reagan. The opinion was that President Reagan held many of the same opinions that he (Pat), the 700 Club, and any born again Christian would have. Pat pledged himself to bringing about social change in America. At the end of the program he was given a message saying that Ronald Reagan was officially in the running for re-election to the office of President of the United States.

The television preachers make it clear where they stand on traditional American values. They also make it plain that they feel these values have been eroded, and they make no "bones" about their commitment to causing the pendulum to swing back to the "old values." While stating they they are committed to no political party, they make it clear that they are in agreement with much of what the political conservatives in the country are saying. It seems pretty clear that they will endorse President Reagan for the office of President again, and they seem to be gathering enough political influence to expect certain things from him. The day after President Reagan announced his candidacy, he spoke to a meeting

of the National Religious Broadcasters; and the day
after that, Pat Robertson spoke to them. President
Reagan, in his State of the Union Address, said that he
would continue to push for legislation against
abortion, and for prayer in school. He said to an
audience of evangelists at the meeting of the National
Religious Broadcasters, "I need the help of people like
you." There are far sweeping changes in store if this
marriage between the television preachers and the
Presidency is successful.

The message for those who join in the television
ministry is to "gird up your loins." When people become
part of the television ministry they are told to take a
stand for God. In 1984, this seems to mean to take a
certain political stand. The success of the "social
gospel" of the television preachers appears to hang on
their political stance. Perhaps the elections will
decide the issue.

The Use of Computer Technology

John answered, saying unto them all, I
indeed baptize you with water; but one
mightier than I cometh, the latchet of
whose shoes I am not worthy to unloose:
he shall baptize you with the Holy Ghost
and with fire: Whose fan is in his hand,
and he will thoroughly purge his floor,
and will gather the wheat into his garner;
but the chaff he will burn with fire
unquenchable.

Luke 3:16-17

We live in the dawning of the computer age in
American society. Today, almost everything we do is
touched, in some way, by that amazing electronic
thinking machine. A computer prints our paychecks (and,
alas, our bills as well), records our taxes, checks the
price of our groceries, sorts our mail, analyzes
mountains of data, and records our birth and death. In
any given year we receive "personal" computer letters

52

from scores of magazines, book clubs, politicians, and charitable organizations. Is it any wonder that the T.V. preachers have caught on to the the idea of using the computer in their ministries?

Any organization that desires to "communicate" with a large number of people needs the modern computer. The mass media ministers are no exception. Of course, the T.V. preachers must have some way to get in touch with potential members before they can bring the full capacity of the computer to bear in communicating with them. The Mass Media Ministers also need some way to ensure the continuing support of existing partners. Essentially, there are two ways that potential members can be contacted: (1) mailing lists of persons believed to be sympathetic to the television ministers can be rented, and (2) those people who watch religious programming can be invited to "call-in" on a toll-free number or a "prayer line," and information can be gathered at that time for a computer follow-up. We will look at the invitation to "call-in" as the primary methods for contacting potentially new members for the television ministry.

January was dubbed "my vote" month on Jim Bakker's PTL Television Network. During this time, anyone watching is asked to contact the PTL Network (by calling or writing) and let Jim know the call-letters of the station, or the name of the cable system, on which the PTL Network is broadcast. As Bakker explains it, the "votes" will be used to "evaluate" the various viewing areas served by PTL. For every person who "casts a vote to keep PTL on the air," Jim will send them a medallion with the inscription "No weapon formed against you shall prosper," on one side, and "God loves you," on the other side. The "gift" is free for simply casting you "vote." We have no reason to doubt that Jim Bakker will use the information on "votes" to evaluate PTL's broadcasting priorities, but we are hard pressed to believe that it is coincidental that those people who "vote" will have their names and addresses entered into PTL's computer data banks. Moreover, those who "voted to keep PTL on the air" will likely receive a personalized, computer generated letter from Jim. In this letter, each "voter" will typically be given the opportunity to make a financial contribution to the ministry, or, if they are so inclined, to pledge fifteen dollars (or more) a month in order to become a partner of the PTL Club. If a person joins, or otherwise contributes to the network, he or she can expect to receive additional "personal" letters from the T.V. preacher. In times of financial crises on the PTL Network, people who "called in their vote," joined the PTL Club, purchased bible or "victory" tapes, or otherwise gave money, will have an opportunity to aid in resolving the financial difficulties of PTL. Those who never respond to appeals for money will soon be dropped from the computer generated mailing list. Of course, this is only sound solicitation practice.

So what, the reader may be asking. There is nothing new, or necessarily sinister, in computer generated mass mailings. We agree; and we are not suggesting that the T.V. ministers are trying to conceal their purposes. Our point is that the marriage of television religion with the computer places the media ministers at a competitive advantage over pastors of traditional, mainline churches. If the reader is a member of a mainline church, ask yourself when you last received a letter from your pastor that began "Dear John, or Dear Mary," and went on to inquire about your progress with a specific illness or other problem. More than likely, the last written communication from your church was a mimeographed newsletter or "messenger," with no personal salutation, and no reference to you as an individual at all. Compare the two communication forms, and the power of the computer becomes apparent.

The Use of Celebrity Guests

And when thou prayest, thou shalt not be
as the hypocrites are: for they love to pray
standing in the synagogues and in the corners
of the streets, that they may be seen of men.

Matthew 6:5

Anyone who watches television knows that big-name, celebrity guests greatly enhance the appeal of a program. This is particularly true of news programs, talk shows, soap operas and other forms of programming that the television industry has to offer. It is also true of the television ministers, and the T.V. preachers utilize this interest getting measure as a means to enhance their programs. Many portions of the 700 Club and the PTL Club are very similar to a commercial television talk show. The format of these shows remind us of the Johnny Carson show and the like. They usually have guests who are very familiar to the viewing audience. These guests are interviewed in an atmosphere of informality; more often then not, they are from the entertainment industry.

We have seen Pat Boone and his family on PTL; Pearl Bailey has also been a guest on Jim Bakker's PTL Club show. Roy Rogers and Dale Evans make frequent appearances on television church programs. Various prominent television preachers appear together on these shows. There are also people from a variety of other professions, including psychologists, authors of Christian books, politicians, and business executives. The conversations naturally are carried on in the context of the religious commitment of the guests, and their born again experiences. The importance of these famous people giving a personal testimony about their religious commitment is certainly not missed by the viewing public.

These guests typically praise the importance of the television ministry, often urging the viewer to get involved in the television ministry. Many of them demonstrate their personal support for the television church. During a recent membership drive held by the 700 Club of Pat Robertson, Dale Evans Rogers joined the one thousand dollar club by handing Pat a check for that amount. Periodically, during the interviews of famous guests, a toll-free number is flashed at the bottom of the television screen. The viewer can call that number and pledge money in either one-time gifts or by joining that particular television ministry. In the chapter on the growth of the television ministries, we will trace the growth of these various television churches from their beginning to the present. The amount of money they raise through the members who give to their ministry is large indeed. The use of famous-name people on these programs undoubtedly helps to attract interest and to raise money. This is further reinforced by the spots shown of ordinary people who are giving their money to the television ministry.

Give and You Shall Receive

And Jesus answering said unto them, Render
to Cesar the things that are Cesar's, and
to God the things that are God's.

Mark 12:17

        The people who watch the television church, and
who choose to support one of the television preacher's
ministries, number in the millions in the United
States. When they begin to give their financial support
to television churches, they join a large group of
people who are already members. Of the many short
testimonies given by ordinary folks who join, the
persons usually say something like, "I know my small
amount does not seem significant, but I know that when
it is added to what others are giving, it makes it
possible for the Gospel to be preached." Another
typical testimony is "I have been a member for some
time and I have decided to raise my pledge because God
has blessed my finances." It would be a mistake to
treat these pledges to the television church lightly,
or as a "drop in the bucket," because given enough
drops, "the bucket runneth over." One has to wonder if
the mainline churches look with more than a little
apprehension, and envy, as the "bucket runneth over" on
the Electronic Church. While the television preachers
usually don't pass a plate, they do pass a toll-free
number; a number that touches an audience of potential
givers that is more vast than the audience any church
"offering plate" ever touches.

        In a fund-raising drive at the end of January,
1984, the 700 Club enlisted the pledges of over 90,000
new members. The total amount pledged, as the tension
built up during the final minutes of the telethon, was
5.2 million dollars. It should be noted that this was
5.2 million dollars a month!

        On the 700 Club show, Pat Robertson gives frequent
talks on how a person can have financial success; he

advises people to tear up their credit cards, to quit
paying high interest rates, and to live within their
means. He tells about a principle he calls the "law of
reciprocity." This law maintains that as a believer
gives to the work of the Kingdom of God, he or she will
receive blessings from God which will far outweigh what
was originally given. Quite actually, one hears that
one way to give to God's work is to join the 700 Club.
One can join the 700 Club by calling the toll-free
number that is flashed on the T.V. screen and pledging
fifteen dollars a month, or by joining the $1000 Club,
or, for those committed Christians who will step out in
faith, by joining the $2500 Club. The 700 Club gets
many calls during its broadcasts from people who say
that they have "stepped out in faith," not knowing how
they were going to keep their pledge. Many report that
as they gave, and as they prayed, miraculous things
began to happen in their financial affairs. The
"blessed financial events" include such things as
failing businesses being restored to success, bills
being paid that seemed impossible to pay, and money
coming in from unexpected sources.

On Jim Bakker's PTL Club, viewers are invited to
become PTL Partners by calling the toll-free number
(1-800-CALL-JIM), and pledging fifteen dollars a month
to the Bakker ministry. In doing this, the believer is
told that he or she is becoming a part of the work of
God in America, and in the world. The sense of
belonging is reinforced for the believer by stressing
the principle that, as they become members, they become
part of the larger "Body of Christ"-- people who are
participating in the ministry of the PTL Club. And, we
call attention to the fact that Jim Bakker and Pat
Robertson are not unique in using this method of
getting financial support from their ministries. Jimmy
Lee Swaggart, using the same procedures, raised over 60
million dollars for his ministry. Almost all of the
television preachers, when the contents of their
appeals are analyzed, use these, or some variant, of
these methods.

The frequency and fervency of the appeals can be
understood from the very logistics of the television
church. It takes a lot of money to operate a satellite
and to carry out all of the ministries in which the
T.V. preachers, and their organizations, are involved.
Later in this book, when we trace the growth of the
television church, we will see that this growth has

necessitated ever-increasing budgets. While the television preachers raise money in many other ways, the faithful, through giving, provide the mass media ministers with a large portion of their huge budgets.

When the T.V. preachers make their appeals, they cite many passages from the Bible to support their belief that God returns to the giver many spiritual and physical blessings. The passages they frequently refer to are many, and include the story of Jesus feeding 5000 people, starting with just five fish and two loaves (Mt. 14:13-21; Mk. 6:30-44; Lk. 9:10-17; and John 6:1-4), Jesus teaching about anxiety (Lk. 12:32-34),and Jesus' parable about the use of talents (Mt. 25:14-30). The list could go on. On balance, the main point the preachers stress from these passages is tht God blesses the believer who is also a giver. Thus, the television preachers have a sound Biblical grounding in using these sections of scripture. As we have seen, millions of dollars are raised as a result of these appeals. The cycle, of needing more money, getting more money, expanding, and needing more money, goes on and on in the television ministry.

There are many people in this country who are cynical about the methods used by the T.V. preachers and the use to which the money they raise is put. But we should not forget that there are many people who are not cynical, and who demonstrate their belief in the work of the television preachers by voting with their pocketbooks for the television ministry.

THE SUBJECT OF VERACITY

And the scribes and the Pharisees brought unto
him a woman taken in adultery; and when they had
set her in the midst, They say unto him, Master,
this woman was taken in adultery, in the very act.
Now Moses in the law commanded us, that such should
be stoned: but what sayest thou? This they said,
tempting him, that they might have to accuse him.
But Jesus stooped down, and with his finger wrote
on the ground, as though he heard them not. So
when they continued asking him, he lifted up
himself, and said unto them, He that is without sin
among you, let him first cast a stone at her.

John 8:3-7

As we have outlined and discussed the several methods used by the media ministers to create and maintain their prime time partners, we have tried to avoid casting stones in the direction of the T.V. ministers. There have been, are today, and will be tomorrow, an ample supply of critics of religious broadcasters in America. Joining with these critics and the already long entourage of "doubting Thomas'" is not our goal. We have tried to describe the methods and the apparent goals of the television preachers as we understand them. Clearly, we have no way of "getting inside" the minds of the media ministers and discovering their "true" goals, desires, and aspirations. We have wondered, however, through what process those people who do claim to "know" the honesty and integrity of the T.V. preachers actually acquire that knowledge.

A number of years ago the sociologist W.I. Thomas suggested that "situations that are defined as real are real in their consequences." Other sociologists have pointed out that we human beings live and function in a "reality" that is defined by the perspective we bring to it. If this is true, and a great deal of sociological research gives strong support to that conclusion, we need to try to understand the perspectives of the T.V. preachers, instead of evaluating what they say and what they do from the standpoint of conventional wisdom and values of traditional, mainline churches. In doing so we may find that the critics of the T.V. preachers are fully justified in their critical remarks. We should not, however, rule out the possibility that their critical remarks are wholly without foundation. One thing is certain, there has not been a lot of effort spent in an attempt to understand the media ministers. There is a second certainty; if we attempt to understand, rather than simply negatively characterize the television ministers, we may just learn something important about them, as well as the people they lead and influence. We could certainly do worse than that.

CASTING THE NET: PREACHING TO "WHO-SO-EVER" WILL

CASTING THE NET: PREACHING TO "WHO-SO-EVER" WILL

INTRODUCTION

Again, the devil taketh him up to an exceeding
high mountain, and sheweth him all the kingdoms
of the world, and the glory of them; and saith
unto him, all these things I will give thee, if
thou wilt fall down and worship me. Then saith
Jesus unto him, Get thee hence, Satan: for it is
written, Thou shalt worship the Lord thy God, and
him only shalt thou serve.

Matthew 4:8-10

Who are the people who watch Christian television? Do
they walk around in sack cloth? Are they all "poor
little retiring Christians?" Do they all speak in
tongues, handle snakes, or stand on street corners
preaching the "Good News?" Hardly! The people who watch
Christian television cut across the entire spectrum of
American society. They are upper class, middle class,
and lower class. They are Caucasion, Black, American
Indian, Hispanic, and others. They are female, and they
are male. They are well educated and they are poorly
educated. They are young, middle aged, and they are
elderly. They are in good health and they are in poor
health. They are Southern Baptist, Methodist,
Presbyterian, Episcopalian, Lutheran, Roman Catholic,
American Baptists, and people of other faiths. We
believe that it is important for the reader to
understand that to characterize people who watch
Christian television as "fundamentalist,"
"charismatic," "evangelical,"or "pentecostal," does not

automatically imply a group of people who are lower class, powerless, or uninvolved and unconcerned with societal events. In other words, the people who watch religious television are from diverse social and economic backgrounds, and they are an important force in American society.

When the reader watches and listens to the T.V. church, he or she may get the impression that the Mass Media Members are all very prosperous. For example, during his telethon for the PTL Satellite Network, Jim Bakker stated that of all the families that visited Heritage Village during 1983, their average annual family income was $36,000.While we do not know which particular "average" Bakker was using, we feel certain that the "arithmetic average" of all of those who send money to the Bakker ministries is substantially less than $36,000 per year. One thing is certain, PTL Partners, "Faith Partners," 700 Club and Eagle Club members are willing to spend their money on the television church.While their social statuses are varied, the majority of those who watch the T.V. church do, nevertheless, share some common characteristics. We propose to outline those common characteristics in this chapter.

There are many correlates of religious commitment that can be discussed and explored. We have in mind such factors as gender, age, education, and geographical region of residence. As we describe and discuss these differences, we will be providing an outline of the social and economic characteristics of the bulk of the audience of the Mass Media Ministers. Much of the information we will use in our discussion is based on research conducted by the Gallup organization.

SOCIAL CORRELATES OF MASS MEDIA MEMBERS

And Jesus, walking by the sea of Galilee, saw
two brethren, Simon called Peter, and Andrew his
brother, casting a net into the sea: for they
were fishers. And he saith unto them, follow me
and I will make you fishers of men. And they
straightaway left their nets, and followed him.

Matthew 4:18-20

Gender: Mass Media Ministers and Mom

And the angel said unto her, Fear not, Mary: for
thou hast found favour with God.

Luke 1:30

Social scientists have long accepted the idea that
females are more religious than males. We are not
saying that social scientists simply agree, or
"believe" that women are more religious than men; their
conclusions are based on the results of research
covering a period of well over fifty years.1
Differences between males and females on religious
commitment are among the most consistent of all
findings in the scientific study of religion. In
American society, the most notable exceptions to this
general rule are to be found among members of the
Jewish and Mormon faiths.2 In these two religious
groups, males are equally or more religious than
females (when church attendance is used as a measure of
religious commitment).3

A key factor in any discussion of personal religious
commitment is the extent to which a person considers
his or her religious beliefs to be personally
important. If females are more religious than males, we
would expect a higher percentage of women to consider
their religious beliefs to be "very important."
According to Gallup, sixty-six percent of the female
respondents, and forty-seven percent of the male
respondents said that their personal religious beliefs
were "very important" to them. In addition, a higher
percentage of females expressed the belief that
religion is "increasing its influence in American
life." While forty-four percent of the females
expressed this belief, only thirty-five percent of the
males stated such a belief.

Also, seventy-three percent of females, and sixty-five percent of males say that they believe in life after death. As regards having confidence in organized religion, forty-seven percent of the female respondents report having a "great deal of confidence" in organized religion, while forty-one percent of the males do so. When asked about their interpretation of the Bible, forty-seven percent of the females, as compared to thirty-three percent of the males, indicated that describing the Bible as the "actual word of God" came closest to their own feelings about the Bible. Other studies have found women to be more religious than men on such things as prayer, conservative beliefs, church identification, church attendance, interest in religion, acceptance of religious doctrine, involvement in church activities, orthodoxy, and others.5 Females, it seems, even read religious literature more than males; Newsweek recently reported that "85 percent of the patrons of Christian bookstores are women."6

During a recent visit to Jim Bakker's Heritage Village USA, we were impressed with the employees of PTL and with the grounds of Heritage Village. We were also impressed with the number of female visitors we saw, as contrasted with the number of male visitors. During a forty-five minute stay in the "Upper Room," approximately 20 people came into the Upper Room-- only one was male. On Saturday evening we attended the "Camp Meeting USA" service held in the "Big Barn" auditorium at Heritage Village USA, and we estimated that between 70 and 80 percent of those in attendance were female. However, this particular Saturday service was not well attended-- the auditorium was less than 25 percent full. We mention this to point out that this service may have been atypical, and our observations of the percent of the audience that was female should be interpreted with caution. Nevertheless, most of the people who watch Christian television are older females. During the several hundred hours we have spent (and continue to spend) watching the television preachers, we have made every effort to keep track of the distribution of males and females in the audiences of the various preachers. Whether it is Jim Bakker's PTL Club, Pat Robertson's 700 Club, Jimmy Swaggart's crusades, Robert Schuller's "Hour of Power," Jerry Savelle's "Adventures in Faith," Kenneth Copeland's crusades, Rex Humbard, Oral and Richard Roberts, Lester Sumrall, Jerry Bernard, John Ankerberg, or John and

66

Anne Gimenez, we always count many more females than males in the audience. Of those females we count, most are middle-age, or older.

We feel that we should point out that the T.V. preachers did not make females the largest segment of their viewing audiences. It would not be reasonable to suggest that the Mass Media Ministers target women any more than it would be safe to level such an accusation at the traditional, mainline church in America. Social scientific data clearly show that women are the membership "backbone" of the mainliners, regardless of denomination (except for Jews and Mormons). Given this data, we should not be surprised that the historical distribution of men and women in the traditional church would also be reflected in the viewing audience of Christian television. While the T.V. preachers did not make women the bulk of their viewers, the obverse may be true-- females may have played a large part in making the T.V. preachers what they are today.

We do not want to give the impression that the T.V. preachers are unaware of the importance of females to the continuing support of their ministries. The Mass Media Ministers are intelligent men, not intellectual simpletons who preach simple, easy-to-understand messages because they are incapable of complex thinking. An unintelligent person could not, it seems to us, create, maintain, and administer the complex bureaucracies these men have built. So it is reasonable to assume that they know of the overwhelming female support of their operations. On a recent telecast of the Jim Bakker Show, Bakker made the statement that "some of the church workers-- who are really busy bodies-- may not be there [heaven]." Now, that is a simple statement, carrying the message that just because one is involved in "church work" does not assure salvation. Of course, the vast majority of those who do the "extra" church work are females. What Bakker seems to be saying to his audience is "stay with us," because mere church work will not get you to heaven. The message is primarily pertinent to women. As we have said repeatedly throughout this book, having a "born again" experience is of fundamental importance to the message of the Mass Media Ministers. When Gallup asked if the individual has had a "born again" experience, thirty-nine percent of the females, and twenty-eight percent of the males, answered affirmatively. Using this basic criteria of the T.V. preachers, it seems to us that females are the most likely candidates to become Mass Media Members of the television church. We must admit, however, that it is one thing for a person to say they are "born again," and quite another thing to openly, and actively, proclaim one's "born again" status to other people. One way of doing so is to "Witness" to others. As Gallup puts it, "witnessing" occurs when an individual tries "to encourage someone to believe in Jesus Christ or to accept Him as his or her Savior." When Gallup asked his respondents if they had "Witnessed" to others, fifty-four percent of the females said yes, and forty percent of the males indicated they had "Witnessed." Given the percentage of women who are "born again," and the percentage who have "Witnessed," we believe there should be no surprise in the statement that the Mass Media Ministers appeal primarily to females. If confirmation is needed for this assertion, we point out that Jeffrey Hadden and Charles Swann report that among the top ten programs on the T.V. church, "the percentage of females in the audience ranges from a low of 60 percent for `Gospel Singing Jubilee' to a high of 73 percent for 'The PTL Club.'"7 For the still unconvinced readers, we simply invite them to watch television religion and count for themselves.

Age: The Closer You Get

And there appeared unto him an angel of the
Lord standing on the right side of the altar
of incense. And when Zacharias saw him, he
was troubled, and fear fell upon him. But
the angel said unto him, Fear not, Zacharias:
for thy prayer is heard, and thy wife
Elisabeth shall bear thee a son, and thou
shalt call his name John.

Luke 1:11-13

The Mass Media Ministers seem to have a special attraction for females in our society. They also seem to have greater appeal to those who are further along in years than to those who are young. During a recent

PTL Telethon to raise money for the new "PTL Partner Center," Reverend Bakker delivered a sermon on turning a life crisis into a miracle. After the sermon he gave the call for viewers to say "the sinners prayer" with him, and then to phone and "confess Jesus with their mouths" to make their salvation complete. We mention this because after asking people to call, the "counselors" on the toll-free number (1-800-CALL-JIM) and/or the prayer line number (1-704-554-6000)--all 150 of them --were jammed with people calling-in. What was remarkable about those who called-in was their age (as reported by Jim Bakker); as we counted them, over seventy percent of the callers were in the 60, 70, and 80 year old category. Even Jim Bakker was surprised at the large percentage of the elderly "coming" to Christ."

We do not pretend to suggest that over seventy percent of the mass media members are sixty years of age, or older. We do intend, however, to suggest that it is likely that viewers of Christian television do tend to be older, rather than younger.

As we pointed out earlier, the Mass Media Ministers use the "born again" experience as a basic criterion for calling someone a "Christian." When asked if they would say that they have been "`born again' or have had a `born again' experience-- that is, a turning point in your life when you committed yourself to Christ," twenty-nine percent of those 18-29 years old, said "yes." As the ages of the respondents increased, however, the percentage affirming a "born again" experience also increased, to wit: of those 30-49 years old, thirty-three percent answered "yes," and of those 50 years of age and over, thirty-nine percent reported a "born again" experience.

We also pointed out earlier that we recognize that there is an important difference between being "born again" and keeping it a private matter unto oneself, and announcing one's "born again" status publicly. When we look at the relationship between "witnessing" and age, we find that as age increases, the incidence of "witnessing" also increases. In response to the Gallup poll, forty-one percent of those 18-29 said they have witnessed, forty-four percent of those 30-49 have witnessed, and fifty-four percent of those 50 and over indicated they have witnessed.

We see a similar pattern as regards age and religiousness on the remaining questions which we discussed earlier for males and females. Looking at responses to the question, "How important to you are your religious beliefs," we find that sixty-three percent of those 50 and over described their personal religious beliefs as "very important." For those people 30-49, fifty-eight percent answered "very important," and of those under 30, thirty-five percent chose that answer. The pattern repeats itself regarding "confidence in organized religion," interpretation of the Bible," and belief in "immortality."

It is not very difficult to understand the peculiar attraction of Christian television for those who are getting along in years. Advancing age brings a number of life circumstances with it, especially for people in the lower socio-economic classes, which are often difficult to manage. Loneliness, financial insecurity, failing health, and impending death are among the most obvious. The T.V. preachers have a message for each of these conditions of the aging and the elderly.

For those whose children have left the nest, whose husband (or wife) has died, or who have no family at all, the message is to "accept Christ," be "born again," and loneliness will no longer be a problem. Again, the Mass Media Ministers are on solid Biblical ground in taking such a position. We are reminded of the last words of the "great commission," when Jesus said "and, lo, I am with you alway, even unto the end of the world (Matthew 28:20)."

If the T.V. preachers have a second "great commission" (other than preaching the Gospel), it is raising money to carry the "good news" throughout the world. Of course, to legitimate their own appeals for money, the T.V. preachers must make financial success and security Biblically available to the people who watch their programs. It is no accident , therefore, that the T.V. preachers almost always tie a viewer's financial security to "giving" to the television ministry. In a recent telethon in which one of the goals was to raise 30 million dollars to build a "world class hotel" to make it possible for "God's people" to "fellowship together," Jim and Tammy Bakker read many testimonials of people being "blessed financially" because they gave to PTL. It is not unusual for the T.V. preachers to report on people who received $10,000

70

almost immediately after pledging just $1,000 to the television ministry. In the January/February, 1983, issue of the PTL Partner magazine, "Together," Jim Bakker wrote about receiving financial security through giving to God's work. He entitled his article "How to Have an Abundant Harvest." According to Jim Bakker:8

> If you want God's blessing, the first thing you have to do is stop looking at circumstances.Stop worrying about the financial situation of the world around you and start exercising your faith in God.

Bakker went on to ask:

> Do you want to get ahead? Are you tired of living on the edge of financial disaster? Then start living by God's universal law of prosperity. Start planning your harvest by planting your seeds of faith. Give your money, your talents, your time, your love, yourself. Give to God by giving to others.

> When you do, I guarantee God's going to give you a harvest so big you won't have room to receive it. You'll be begging people to take money from you because God has blessed you so much.

Is there a Biblical basis for Bakker's position on giving and subsequent blessings? Again, the answer is, yes. Jim Bakker, and the other T.V. preachers, usually refer to Luke 6:38, where Jesus said:

> Give, and it shall be given unto you; good measure, pressed down, and shaken together, and running over, shall men give unto your bosom.For with the same measure that ye mete withal it shall be measured to you again.

Can one give to the Mass Media Ministers and be giving to God's work? According to the T.V. preachers you can; and if one does give to Christian television, one can expect important and significant financial blessings to follow.

As a person's age marches inexorably onward and upward, health problems of both minor and major proportions become more common. Many of these difficulties can be treated, but not cured by modern medicine. It is in these circumstances that the healing ministries of the Mass Media Ministers have a special appeal to the elderly. While it is easy to understand the unique attraction of the healing ministry for the aging, we must point out that the T.V. preachers do not "target" that segment of the population. Pat Robertson, Jim Bakker, Oral Roberts, and other television ministers frequently report miraculous, supernatural healings that have taken place in the lives of infants, the very young, young adults, and those of middle age, as well as among the elderly. It is, nevertheless, not difficult to grasp the special appeal of spiritual healing for the elderly. The message is not a complex one; in fact, it is as simple as believing that Jesus died on the Cross and rose from the dead. If the viewer believes, then he or she is assured that "by his stripes ye are healed."

Based on our discussion so far, we conclude that the most likely candidates to become viewers of T.V. religion are females. Additionally, it appears that as one grows older, one's attachment to religion makes one a better candidate to watch Christian television. A word of caution is in order here; we are not saying that all of those who watch the T.V. preachers are both female and older. We have already pointed out that those who watch religious television are from diverse social and economic backgrounds. However, an examination of available data does suggest that females, and not males, people who are older, and not younger, represent the largest portion of the potential audience for Mass Media Ministers.

We can be even more specific in our description of those people who represent the bulk of the potential audience for the T.V. preachers. To do so, we will examine education and region of residence as additional correlates of religious commitment in American society.

Education: And the Last Shall be First

Fear not, little flock; for it your Father's good pleasure to give you the kingdom. Sell what ye have, and give alms; provide yourselves

bags which wax not old, a treasure in the
heavens that faileth not, where no thief
approacheth, neither moth corrupteth. For where
your treasure is, there will your heart be also.

Luke 12:32-34

In considering level of education as a correlate of
religious commitment, we will again begin with those
two criteria most important to the television
preachers-- having a "born again" experience and
"witnessing." Education is broken down into the three
categories of college, high school, and grade school.
Of those who have an educational level corresponding to
"college," twenty-seven percent indicate having had a
"born again" experience. For those with a "high school"
education, thirty-six percent have been "born again"
and, for those with a "grade school" education,
forty-two percent have been "born again." Clearly, as
education increases, the likelihood of having a "born
again" experience decreases, and so does the potential
for becoming a regular and frequent viewer of Christian
television.

Again, however, the "acid test" may very well be the
willingness of a person to "witness" to their "born
again" status. When we look at the responses concerning
"witnessing," we are very impressed with the
relationship between education and being willing to
"encourage someone to believe in Jesus Christ or to
accept Him" as one's personal Savior. Of those people
who reported a grade school education, a very high
sixty-five percent said they had "witnessed." By
comparison, only thirty-seven percent of those with a
college education reported having "witnessed." For
those who have a high school education, forty-seven
percent report having "witnessed." Clearly, the group
least likely to be what Jim Bakker has called "closet
Christians" are those in the lower levels of
educational attainment in American society.

Sociologists, psychologists, philosophers, and
religionists, have characterized religious orientations
into two basic types: (1) "other worldly" orientations,
and (2) "this worldly" orientations. Interestingly,
there is a well documented relationship between social
class and the type of religious orientation with which

a person is likely to associate. In general, the higher the social class, the greater the probability of association with a religion that has a "this worldly" orientation and, the lower the social class, the greater the likelihood of association with a religion that has an "other worldly" orientation.

While religions with an "other worldly" orientation do talk about financial success and job security in the present life, their primary emphasis is on the rewards to come in the after-life in God's kingdom. In "other worldly" religions it is unusual to hear sermons dealing with abstract theology, or complex moral positions. The typical emphasis is on accepting Jesus Christ as one's personal Savior, confessing one's "born again" status openly, being filled with the Holy Spirit, and dedicating one's life to "winning" others to the enduring love of Christ. If one does these things, one can look forward to ascending to heaven and dwelling there in the presence of the Lord. To make the ideology meaningful, "other worldly" religions emphasize certain aspects of Holy Scripture. It is no accident that these religions emphasize, and reemphasize such scriptures as "the meek shall inherit the earth," and "the first shall be last and the last shall be first." If a person is not well educated, it is unlikely that he or she will have a white collar, professional, or technical occupation. It is also unlikely that such a person will experience high earnings during their lifetime. Whether we like it or not, the quality of life is related to these three factors-- income, education, and occupation, and those in the lower echelons of these factors do not usually live lives of great comfort and ease. We should not be surprised, therefore, that people in the lower socio-economic classes would feel most comfortable with an "other worldly" religious orientation, an orientation which emphasizes that although their life circumstances are less that satisfactory now, they will receive a heavenly reward that the "rich" will find most difficult to attain. In fact, they will be "first" in the kingdom of heaven. "This worldly" religions focus their attention on rewards that are obtainable in this earthly life. We should not be surprised that such religions appeal primarily to members of the middle and upper classes. It would make little sense for those people who do not live in fine houses, wear fashionable, name brand clothes, drive new automobiles, send their children to the "better" schools, or take elaborate vacations, to be attracted to a religious orientation which suggests that success, prosperity, and material things are evidence of God's blessings upon their earthly life. What we have reference to is the whole notion of Calvanistic presdestination as it is embodied in the Protestant work-ethic.

On the other hand, people who are relatively comfortable in this life find a great deal of affectivity for religions with a "this worldly" orientation. Why should they be concerned with the idea that "the meek shall inherit the earth"-- they already own it!

So those who are less well educated are more likely to subscribe to an "other worldly" religious orientation. Anyone who spends just one or two evenings watching the Mass Media Ministers will have all of the documentation needed to confirm that the T.V. preachers operate from a theological position with a strong "other worldly" orientation. Clearly, such an orientation ministers to those who are less well educated than most of middle and upper class America.

Once again, however, we feel that we must point out that the T.V. preachers are not, in our opinion, exploiting the known social stratum that their viewers occupy. On the contrary, it is our position that the television ministers preach what they actually believe. A quick check of the socio-economic backgrounds of the Mass Media Ministers will show that they were, by and large, socialized in much the same sort of social milieu as those who watch their programming today. Whatever the reasons (and we are aware that many others could be advanced), the evidence is rather clear that those people who watch, regularly and frequently, the Mass Media Ministers, are typically not as well educated as those who do not watch. Given this fact, coupled with what is known about the educational attainment of the various regions of the country, it is instructive to ask if the regular viewers of Christian television are concentrated in certain areas of the United States.

In view of our discussion thus far,we conclude that the largest segment of the Christian television audience is composed of older females who are rather poorly educated. Where do these people live? Are they evenly distributed throughout the society? Is the message of the Mass Media Ministers as loud in California as it is in Nebraska, or Maryland, or Alabama? Are the T.V. preachers ministering to each region of America equally? The answer to these questions is "no." Like any other T.V. program, the Mass Media Ministers appeal to certain segments of the population. We will now consider where those particular segments are most likely to reside.

Region of Residence: You Can Make It!

There cometh a woman of Samaria to draw water: Jesus saith unto her, Give me to drink. (For his disciples were gone away unto the city to buy meat). Then saith the woman of Samaria to him, How is that thou, being a Jew, askest drink of me, which am a woman of Samaria? for the Jews have no dealings with the Samaritans. Jesus answered and said unto her, If thou knewest the gift of God, and who it is that saith to thee, Give me to drink: Thou wouldest have asked of him, and he would have given thee living water.

John 4:7-10

In considering region of residence, we will once again concentrate on the two basic criteria of the T.V. preachers, that is, being "born again" and "witnessing." And again, available data prove to be very revealing as we break region of residence down into those who reside in the "West," the "East," the "Midwest," and the "South."

When asked if they would say that they have been "born again," twenty percent of those who lived in the West responded affirmatively. This compares with twenty-three percent of those in the East, thirty-four percent of those in the Midwest, and fifty-five percent of those in the South. In other words, only one-fifth of the people living in the West have been "born again," while over one-half of those residing in the South are "born again" Christians!

Application of "witnessing" as a litmus test reveals a pattern similar to the "born again" pattern. Of those living in the West, thirty-five percent have "witnessed," while of the residents of the East, thirty-eight percent report having "witnessed." In the Midwest, forty-eight percent say they have "witnessed," and sixty-three percent of the residents of the South say that they have "witnessed!" Thus, it seems rather clear that the region of the country in which the Mass Media Ministers are most likely to have sympathetic viewers is the South.

Our profile of the social and economic characteristics of mass media ministers then, looks like this: they are predominately female, older rather than younger, poorly rather than highly educated, and more than likely from the Southern part of America. Table One summarizes the profile.

Before the reader concludes that the T.V. preachers are preying on the weak, the unfortunate, the dispossessed, and the poor, we would want to remind the reader to whom Jesus directed his ministry and teachings. In the Gospel according to St. Luke (18:9-14), "And he spake this parable unto certain which trusted in themselves that they were righteous, amd despised others: Two men went up into the temple to pray; the one a Pharisee stood and prayed thus with himself, God, I thank thee, that I am not as other men are, extortioners, unjust, adulterers, or even as this publican. I fast twice in the week, I give tithes of all that I possess. And the publican, standing afar off, would not lift up so much as his eyes unto heaven, but smote upon his breast, saying, God be merciful to me a sinner. I tell you, this man went down to his house justified rather than the other: for every one that exalteth himself shall be abased; and he that humbleth himself shall be exalted." It seems to us that in carrying out their perception of the "great commission," the Mass Media Ministers are preaching to the very people of whom Jesus spoke of the Gospel according to Luke.

We also do not wish to imply that the T.V. preachers slant their messages toward, or appeal only to those people who are at the bottom of the socio-economic heap. They consistently say that the need for salvation, the need to be born again, is for everyone-- for "who-so-ever." In the parable of the Pharisee and

TABLE ONE+

A Profile of Potential Viewers of Religious Television

	Have Been "Born Again"	Have Witnessed
GENDER		
Men	28%	40%
Women	39*	54*
EDUCATION		
College	27	37
High school	36	47
Grade school	42*	65*
AGE		
18-29 years	29	41
30-49 years	33	44
50 and over	39*	54*
REGION		
West	20	35
East	23	38
Midwest	34	48
South	55*	63*

+Source| Cited in Jackson W. Carroll, Douglas W. Johnson, and Martin E. Marty, Religion in America, New York: Harper and Row, 1979.

the tax collector, the contrast is not between financial and social success (or the lack of it), but rather, between being unwilling or willing to accept the need for forgiveness of sins. In the many hours we have spent watching the T.V. preachers, we have noticed that they insist that forgiveness of sin and the born again experience is for all persons, quite apart from their particular position in the American social class system.

The typical viewer of T.V. religion is an older female, not as well educated as a member of the middle class, and more than likely resides in the Southern region of the United States. If these characteristics are correct-- and evidence suggests that they are, one might be tempted to conclude that those who watch the Mass Media Ministers are an insignificant minority in American society. We agree that they are a minority; the majority of Americans do not watch Christian television. We would not, however, agree that these people are an insignificant segment of our society. Nor, apparently, would the Mass Media Ministers accept such a conclusion.

It is clear that President Reagan doesn't consider them to be unimportant. Although we have been aware of Ronald Reagan's solicitation of the T.V. preachers support, we were, nevertheless, surprised to see the President appear on Jim Bakker's PTL Club, Pat Robertson's 700 Club, and Jerry Falwell's "Spiritual State of the Union" address (on videotape). But the President did appear, and he made an appeal for the support of "born again" Christians for his constitutional amendment to "return prayer to our public schools." Jim Bakker, Pat Robertson, Jimmy Swaggart, Oral Roberts, Rex Humbard, Robert Schuller, James Robison, and other T.V. preachers can, on an almost daily basis, be seen and heard praising President Reagan as an honest, upright, moral, and, most importantly, Godly, Christian man. All of this seems to tell us that although the viewers of Christian television are currently a minority in America, they are certainly an important and, apparently, a politically powerful minority.

TELEVISION RELIGION: POTENTIAL FOR GROWTH

   Are   these   T.V.   Christians   a stable, growing, or a
shrinking minority? The evidence suggests that they are
probably   a growing minority. One thing is certain, the
number   of   Americans   that fit a description of a pool
from   which   new   viewers can be recruited, is growing.
Consider the following evidence:

        1.   The   percent   of   the   population that is
        fifty   years of age or older has increased by
        18.4 percent between 1970 and 1980;

        2.   Those   states experiencing the most rapid
        pooulation   growth are in what is referred to
        as the "sunbelt";

        3.   The   number   of females in the population
        has   increased   from   104   million in 1970 to
        approximately 116.5 million in 1980.

   These data alone   are sufficient to see the potential
for   growth   in the percent of the U.S. population that
watches   T.V.   religion.   There is, however, additional
data   that   can   be used to support the contention that
Christian   television will more than likely continue to
grow.

   The Bureau of Labor Statistics has developed an index
that defines the social classes in American in terms of
range   of   income.   Because   we do not wish to bury the
reader in mountains of statistical data, we will simply
point   out   that   between   1978   and   1983, a five year
period, the percent of Americans who were classified as
middle   class   by   the   Bureau   of   Labor   Statistics
decreased   by approximately 13 percent. Using income as
a   measure   of the standard of living, between 1978 and
1983,   75 percent of those in the middle class declined
in   their standard of living. It is also interesting to
note that in 1982, 34.4 million persons lived below the
poverty   line,   representing   15   percent   of   the U.S.
population.   This   is the highest percentage of persons

living below the poverty line in seventeen years! One interpretation that can be given is that we have a shrinking middle class and an expanding lower class class in American society.

We do not want to suggest that all, or even a majority of those people who declined in social class will become viewers of Christian television. Our point is that societal conditions are conducive to significant increases in the number and percent of the population viewing Christian television.

For those who say that T.V. religion has already reached the "outer limits" of its influence, we beg to disagree. For those who suggest that if simply ignored it will disappear, we suggest that they dare not close their eyes. The T.V. preachers have planted their "seed faith" concurrently with the demise of liberal theology and the outward manifestations of a "revival of God" in the middle of Harvey Cox's "Secular City."Sociologists, psychologists, and others have expressed the opinion that the nature of the religion being offered by the T.V. preachers is simple, shallow, mundane and pedesterian. For example, in a recent television course on Introductory Sociology aired on PBS, the narrator opined that Christian television conveys an intellectually oversimplified version of reality. It was further suggested that such a message is potentially dangerous in a modern, technologically advanced society. We cannot disagree. But we are not quite ready to claim that what is superficial to us is also superficial to everyone else. It may be that the message of the T.V. preachers is highly simple, but we agree with the Church Historian Martin Marty that "at heart, the Christian message is simple."

It is difficult to judge, with any certainity, the peculiar attraction of the T.V. preachers for the viewers of Christian television. Are these people attracted to the T.V. preachers because of religion, or because the religion is presented on a medium with which they have become comfortable? In other words, is the attraction religion or is it television? Some sociologists, and communication experts as well, have suggested that the attraction of the T.V. preachers is not traditional religion, but rather, the "religion of television watching" in America. We honestly do not know the answer. Beyond this, however, we do not believe that any other "experts" know the answer

81

either.

We must agree with those sociologists who suggest that some of the T.V. preachers are entertaining-- Jim Bakker, Pat Robertson, and Jimmy Lee Swaggart. It may be true that many viewers who are attracted to these Christian television programs have had their personal "hook" "baited" by the entertainment component of the shows. However, if one is not religious, we believe it would not take a person very long to become saturated with the rather predictable sequence of Christian music, constant testimonials, continual calls to give one's life to Jesus, and the unceasing pleas for money that are characteristic of these shows. Thus, we are of the opinion that the first attraction of the Christian entertainment programs is religion.

It is instructive, we believe, that the "simple" answers of Christian television seem to have a special appeal for a definable demographic category of people in America. It may be that in opting for the simple solution they are choosing the answer of last resort. Is it the right choice? We do not know, but we do know that it is a choice that is being taken. One sociologist with whom we have spoken agreed with the statement that the T.V. preachers are "a stinch in the nostrils of God." Perhaps they are for many people; however, we want to suggest that for many viewers of Christian television the T.V. preachers "smell as sweet as a rose." Given the developing demographics of American society, we believe it is time to "prepare ye the way" of the Mass Media Ministers.

PREACHING TO ALL NATIONS: SATELLITES, GUIDING
LIGHTS, AND BRIGHT STARS

PREACHING TO ALL NATIONS: SATELLITES, GUIDING LIGHTS, AND BRIGHT STARS

INTRODUCTION

Verily, Verily, I say unto you, he that
believeth on me, the works that I do shall
he do also; and greater works than these shall
he do; Because I go unto my father.

John 14:12

In equating greater numbers with greater works, the
television preachers can see themselves fulfilling the
saying of Jesus in the Gospel according to St. John. We
have seen that the 700 Club enlisted over 90,000 new
members on a telethon in January. That number of people
is probably more than all of the people that Jesus and
the disciples preached to in their entire lifetimes
during the founding of Christianity. This has been
possible because of the foresight, and the insight, of
the Mass Media Ministers regarding the use of modern
communications technology. More people have heard the
sermons of the television preachers than the total
number of people who lived on the planet earth in the
first century of Christianity.

The great and influential prophets of the eighth
century B.C. were heard by perhaps a few thousand
people. But it is not unusual for millions of people to

hear, in one hour, the words of the modern-day T.V. prophets. It would take an almost unbelievable stretch of the imagination to believe that the ancient prophets-- Isaiah, Amos, Hosea, and Micah-- could have known, or foreseen, that their teachings would span the continents of the world. Yet today, people in the Judeo-Christian tradition of the Western world hear these words; people in the Muslin tradition of the Middle East hear these words; people in the Hindu tradition of India hear these words; and people who live in traditionally Buddhist cultures hear the words of the Hebrew prophets. All of these people also hear about the writings contained in the New Testament. There are probably more people in Japan who hear the words of St. Paul than he ever preached to in his long ministry. This occurs because the Mass Media Ministers have learned the "tricks of the trade" in the area of mass communications. These include radio, television, satellites, computers, and mass mailings.

The people who spread the Gospel message using these modern, sophisticated methods and techniques, did not begin by using all of the benefits of technology. Practically all of them began in a very modest way, with very little money, and in very humble circumstances. Many began with practically no capital, a limited following, in tents, and often on street corners or in a friendly church. So in this chapter we will trace the growth of the television ministry in its various forms, from its inception to the present. We will point out parallels between the growth of the T.V. ministry and what seems to be a growing interest in religious commitment in the United States. That there is a trend toward increasing interest in religious commitment in this country seems to be supported by Gallup polls conducted in the late 1970's. These polls seem to indicate a growing sense of religious commitment across the spectrum of American society.

In tracing this growth we will not only talk about the raw data, such as the members who give money, the estimated numbers who watch the T.V. church, or the growing budgets of the various ministers, but also about the varied types of programs which are presented on the television church. We will also consider the other forms of income which the television churches have available to continue what they are doing today. In doing so, it will become fairly obvious that the television preachers are exploring, and exploiting areas that the established church has largely ignored. We feel relatively certain that part of the reason for the growth of the television church is that they have learned to address human interests to which the mainline churches have in recent times, given little attention.

In looking at the growth and development of the T.V. preachers, we see an example of what has been termed "the Great American Dream." The television preachers are not ashamed of that dream. Within the context of their theology and their expressed "born again" experience, they say that God intends the highest good for the true believer. In that theology there can be nothing evil, or nothing wrong, with being successful. On the contrary, the T.V. preachers say, "God will help and support those who work for the Kingdom of God in this world." Since this view of the life situation is a part of their position, it is not surprising that the T.V. preachers are going in the direction they have chosen.

THE BASIC MESSAGE

It can be safely said that the television ministers we discuss come from the basic position of Christian fundamentalism. The basic tenets of this position can be found in various places in the Bible and in church history, so they are not new. The term "fundamentalism" is, on the other hand, comparatively new, coming into use around the turn of this century in a particular way that includes five theological concepts: (1) the inerrancy of Scripture, (2) the Diety of Christ, (3) the Virgin Birth of Christ, (4) Christ's blood atonement, and (5) the physical resurrection and personal, bodily return of Christ to earth.

Biblical Inerrancy

When fundamentalists say the Bible is without error, they mean that it is literally God's word, with every passage in it being precisely what God dictated to the writer of a given passage. While the context of a particular passage may place it in a relationship with another passage, or passages of scripture, it

87

nontheless has face validity. By face validity is meant that the passage stands on its own meaning. Further, fundamentalists believe that God has prevented any errors from creeping into the Biblical text over the centuries, even through its many translations and versions. As the Reverend Jerry Falwell put it, "every jot and every tittle is literally true for all time." Thus, the believer can accept scripture as worthy of reverance and as a blueprint for life.

There are, of course, many people who view the Bible as a record of the movement towards a greater understanding of God by Israel and the early church. In this view, the Bible is a record of man's search for God. Not so!, say the fundamentalist television preachers. For them the Bible is the infallible record of God's Self Revelation. Therefore, everyone should love the Bible and give it a central place in their lives. To the T.V. preachers, the Bible is a unified book with one sole author.

The Diety of Christ

The second tenent of fundamentalism states that Jesus Christ was God in the flesh. Therefore, Christ is a part of the God-Head, and is eternal. He participates in every action of God and is therefore worthy of every devotion which can be paid to the Most-High God. One passage, among many which fundamentalists cite in testimony to this belief, is in the gospel of St. John where it says, "that all men should honour the Son, even as they honour the Father. He that honoureth not the Son honoureth not the Father which hath sent him (John 5:23)." Since Jesus is God, his teachings are paramount to any understanding of the nature of God. This is very important to the fundamentalist concept of Christ, in that He was conceived by Mary through the power of the Holy Spirit. Thus, Jesus was born without the original sin of the first man Adam, and all people who came after Adam. As such, Christ was able to be the sacrifical Lamb, without blemish, before God the Father. First and foremost for the fundamentalists, Christ is the "Son of God (Mark 1:11)."

The Virgin Birth

The third belief also has to do with the nature of Jesus. Fundamentalists point to the birth stories in the Gospels of St. Matthew and St. Luke for their authority in believing in the Virgin Birth of Christ. There are some Bible scholars of a liberal bent who say that St. Matthew made a mistake when he quoted the prophet Isaiah as saying "behold a virgin shall be with child, and shall bring forth a son, and they shall call his name Emanual, which being interpreted is, God with us (Matthew 1:23)." These scholars say that Isaiah used the Hebrew word "Almak" which means simply young woman, and not virgin. However, this does not bother fundamentalists since Matthew uses the Greek word for virgin as does Luke. Since for the T.V. preachers the Bible is without error, Jesus was, without a doubt, born of the Virgin Mary.

The Blood Atonement

The doctrine of atonement is an extremely important one to fundamentalist beliefs. It is central to any understanding of this theological position because it incorporates the concepts of man's sin, man's need for forgiveness and mercy, the righteous demands of God for justice, and the idea that since man could not earn his own forgiveness, God had to do it for him. According to the fundamentalists, God granted forgiveness by taking on the likeness of man and dying the death of the cross. When God did this in Christ, He satisfied the demand for justice and punishment for sin, and made it possible for the sinner to be set free.

It is difficult, Biblically speaking, to fault the fundamentalist belief of the T.V. preachers regarding the Doctrine of Atonement. In Cruden's complete concordance, one can find no less that 40 references from the New Testament to Christ's death on the cross, and how this death brings about salvation for man if one will just accept Christ as their Savior and Lord. It is because of this doctrine that the T.V. preachers insist that the Christian life must begin with the "born again experience." While the term "born again"

occurs, in those exact words, only one time in the New
Testament (John 3:3), there are many other cognates in
Scripture. The term "in Christ" was a favorite of St.
Paul. In his Epistles (counting I and II Timothy and
Ephesians as Pauline), we find this term at least 35
times. As used in the Epistles, the term refers to
those who have accepted Christ as Savior, accepted his
death on the cross as true, and who have been "born
again" in the Spirit. So this central belief of
fundamentalist-evangelical preachers is lifted out of
the pages of the earliest documents of the Christian
community. The T.V. preachers simply choose to
emphasize the concept more than many of the mainline
churches.

The Physical Resurrection

The physical resurrection of Christ has also been a
central part of Christian belief since the beginning of
the church. It is embodied in all of the ancient creeds
of the church. I Thessalonians is, by common consensus,
the oldest written document, now extant, in the New
Testament. Thus, when one sees doctrinal statements
grounded in I Thessalonians, one can be sure that one
is seeing some of the beliefs of the early church. In I
Thessalonians mention is made of Christ's death on the
cross and his coming again. It is also stated that
"...the dead in Christ shall rise first (I Thess.,
4:17)." The meaning, according to the T.V. preachers,
is clear-- the letter presupposes the death,
resurrection, and coming again (parousia) of Christ. A
statement in the letter from St. Paul to the church in
Cornith says "and that he was buried, and that he rose
again the third day according to the Scriptures (I
Corinthians 15:4)." In the passages that follow in that
Epistle, the Apostle mentions many people who saw Jesus
Christ after he rose from the dead. Clearly then, this
was a doctrine of the first Christian churches and it
is equally plain that this is a doctrine of the T.V.
preachers. Once again, it should be noted that the
mainline churches also espouse this belief. There has
been, however, some questionning of the physical
resurrection of Christ by scholars of the mainline
churches. No so with the T.V. ministers!

The Mass Media Ministers preach, without compromise,
that the ressurection of Christ was a physical reality

and because of this historical fact, the "born again" believer will rise from the dead when Christ comes again to earth. As with other matters of doctrine, the T.V. preachers will not "water down" what they perceive to be the plain meaning of the Biblical text. This uncompromising attitude seems to us to be a large part of the appeal that the televangelists have for many people. There are apparently lots of folks who do not want their religious experiences or their belief in the Holy explained away by rational arguments. For many people, the experience of the Holy transcends human reason.

The other pole of this belief involves the believer in a very personal way. One can attempt to adopt the Stoic attitude that since death is inevitable, one should view death with detachment. Not many humans do, however. This must of been one of the appeals of the early preaching of the church, and it remains strong in this day of the Electronic church. When we watch a T.V. church service, and see one of the preachers proclaim the coming again of Christ to receive his flock, we cannot help but notice the extremely positive response the preacher gets from his audience.

In outlining these major beliefs of the fundamentalist-evangelical T.V. ministers, we have attempted to demonstrate that these beliefs are shared by all of them. As we discuss the different preachers, the message they present, and the way they present it, the reader should keep in mind not only their commonalities, but differences in personalities and in emphases, as well. The first three men we will mention are, without a doubt, the "guiding lights" of the T.V. church. They have been, and are "guiding lights" to some of the "bright stars" of current-day televangelism, i.e., Jim Bakker, Pat Robertson, Jimmy Swaggart, Jerry Falwell, and many of those we call the "rising stars." The "guiding lights" are the Reverand's Billy Graham, Rex Humbard, and Oral Roberts.

THE "GUIDING LIGHTS"

The Rev. Billy Graham

One could hardly write about T.V. evangelism without talking about the ministry of Dr. Graham. He is one of the pioneers in television, and his crusades have been seen by millions thoughout the world. Recently, in a sociology class composed primarily of college freshmen, we asked the students which T.V. preachers they have watched. The answers given made it clear that all of the students in the class had seen Billy Graham at least once on television. The authors of this book can scarcely remember when they have gone a year without seeing a Billy Graham crusade on television. Part of the reason for his success and public visibility seems to lie in his dynamic preaching over the years.

His preaching style is imposing as well as dynamic. Most people are struck by Dr. Graham's penetrating gaze as he preaches. One is hard-pressed to not be convinced that here is a man who knows his material and is fully committed to what he preaches. He prefaces many of his sermon points with the words "the Bible says." At the core of his preaching is an obvious belief in the inerracy of Scripture and the power of the "Word of God" for salvation. Dr Graham will often raise the Bible high in the air as he makes a point, saying that "this book contains everything you need to know about God's plan for your life." His sermons are typically on the themes which fundamentalists the world over agree upon. The sermons usually have three or four main points, and while the structure of his sermons is simple, the delivery is electric. Dr. Graham has had to slow down some in recent years because of health problems, but when he is delivering a sermon the viewer can still see much of the old fire. Dr. Graham is quick to point out, when asked, that he has no personal charisma because of his own merit, but rather, to quote St. Paul "yet not I but Christ liveth in me (Col., 1:20)." His sermons always include a call to repentance and to accept God's forgiveness and be "born again." His sermons also include a call for people to come forward and publically confess Christ as their savior. Not surprisingly, many do come forward after hearing his emotion-filled, Bible-based sermons. It is also no wonder that many aspiring T.V. evangelists have undoubtedly studied Dr. Graham's sermon content and delivery. He is one of their best role models. It should also be noted that one can see Billy Graham preach only during one of his television crusades. He is not on T.V. on a regular basis as are many of the other preachers.

ORAL
ROBERTS

The Rev. Oral Roberts

Rev. Oral Roberts is widely known in the United States as being a "faith healer." His healing ministry, until recent years, has caused varied reactions among the general public; reactions that have ranged from derision to complete belief in the healing power of God working through Oral Roberts. Roberts dropped his healing ministry for a while, but has recently reinstated it in his telecasts. What many people fail to notice is that Rev. Roberts is, as television preachers go, a first-rate sermonizer.

Roberts nearly always begins his opening remarks by saying "expect a miracle." Once he gets into his sermon he will often remove his coat and preach in shirt-sleeves. This habit probably recalls the days when he was a tent and sawdust floor preacher. He too preaches the standard message of fundamentalism-- repent, and be "born again!" Roberts often adds the message that God will heal any who believe, not only of physical ailments, but also broken relationships and failing finances. He often has his audience repeat phrases after him, and repeat them many times. A typical phrase is one he recently used in a sermon we heard, "God gave us faith in Jesus to give." The people in the audience repeated it several times.

Once again, as in earlier days, he ends the service by healing people in the congregation of various ailments; he also claims healing for people across America who are in the television viewing audience. In one service, he healed a gentleman in the audience of a large lump which the man said had been on his left side for four years. To demonstrate the validity of this healing, Rev. Roberts had the man take off his coat and show the rest of the people that there was no longer a lump there. Many people around the man were saying "Amen," praying, and holding their hands high into the air. Reverend Robert's sermons seem to have taken on a new vitality since he has resumed his healing ministry.

The Rev. Rex Humbard

In Chapter Two we described Rex Humbard as the "Dean" of the television preachers. In this section we will

REX
HUMBARD

examine the man and his ministry more closely.

According to Rex Humbard, he left his father's traveling ministry in 1952. In 1953 he began Calvary Temple in Akron, Ohio, where his ministry remains based today. It seems as though Rex's father, an itinerant preacher, had been conducting one of his tent revivals in Akron in 1952, and while he was there with the revival, Rex had an encounter that was to have profound implications for Humbard in particular, and Christian television, in general. The encounter was not with God, the encounter was not with Jesus, and the encounter was not with the enemy (Satan); the encounter was with one of the scientific marvels of the 20th Century-- Humbard's encounter was with a spirit of the air of a modern sort. What Humbard encountered on that warm summer evening in 1952 was an electronic device receiving audio and video broadcast frequencies-- commonly called a television.1 It seems that the T.V. was on display in a window of O'Neil's Department Store, and folks were gathered around it, transfixed as they watched a baseball game. Humbard reports that it was then and there that he knew television was to become a potent force to be used to carry out the preaching of the "good news" of the new covenant.2

Humbard is a man of average build with a full head of graying hair, and rather typical features. He is married to Maude Aimee, who lends her own musical talent to Rex's services by singing. Rex has several children. When Humbard speaks, he does so with a soft Arkansas drawl and delivers a very simple religious message that is characteristic of basic Christian fundamentalism. It is appropriate that the message is simple, because as far as we can ascertain, Humbard is himself rather uncomplicated. Like the majority of T.V. preachers, Humbard is not extensively educated in a secular, or a religious sense. In his book To Tell The World, Humbard indicates that he has studied courses in the Bible and religion. Perhaps these courses were of the correspondence type, but whatever they were, they were not as far as we can tell, part of an accredited curriculum. In any event, Humbard has been ordained by the International Ministerial Federation, an organization of unaffiliated ministers. Apparently, Humbard has never been formally affiliated with a recognized religious denomination-- his current ministry is unaffiliated.

Humbard's church began in an old movie house which he purchased as the home for "Calvary Temple." In 1958, the "Cathedral of Tomorrow" was completed; a round church that holds 5000 people and was designed specifically with television broadcasting in mind. Like other television preachers, Humbard focuses his preaching on the basic tenets of Christian fundamentalism. Unlike Billy Graham, Humbard emphasizes financial giving to his particular ministry.

Probably as much as any single person, Humbard has pioneered Christian television and paved the way for the "bright stars" of today. In fact, he has been so successful in being a "guiding light" unto the "bright stars" that his own ministry seems to be suffering from the increased competition of the other T.V. preachers. Whatever his own fate, he is clearly one of the "founding fathers" of modern Christian television programming.

We have discussed the "guiding lights" of the T.V. preachers. It is now time to turn our attention to the current "bright stars" of television religion in America. The T.V. preachers we have in mind as the current "bright stars" are Pat Robertson, Jim Bakker, Jimmy Lee Swaggart, Jerry Falwell, and Robert Schuller. Each of these men is different, and each seems to have a specific calling within the general calling of the "great commission." We turn first to the Reverend Jerry Falwell.

MASS MEDIA MINISTERS: THE "BRIGHT STARS"

The Rev. Jerry Falwell

The television ministry of The Reverend Jerry Falwell is a benchmark when one examines the success of the television church. He has been the main motivating force behind the movement called The Moral Majority. But long before he achieved this fame and became a person whom the President of the United States would refer to, he was building a ministry which started literally from "scratch." From a beginning in an abandoned building, which once housed the Donald Duck

97

JERRY
FALWELL

Bottling Company near the Blue Ridge Mountains in Virginia, until today, when his ideas are hailed by many people (including President Reagan), his ministry and influence have been phenomenal.

The Reverend Falwell says that all of the glory for his success belongs to God; a statement with which many people disagree. However, a dispassionate observer of this growth cannot argue with Rev. Falwell's constant expansion. When we look at the graphs provided by the Jerry Falwell Ministries, we find a very impressive uprising in growth during the period between 1966 and 1971. The growth, of course, continues. The graphs which The Reverend Falwell present show the growth in the following areas of his overall program:

1. Income;

2. Television stations reached;

3. Radio stations reached;

4. Membership in the Old Time Gospel Hour;

5. Enrollment in the Liberty Baptist College and schools;

Jerry Falwell has obviously come a long way from an abandoned building to the founding of the Moral Majority. In 1981, he had a total of four hundred T.V. stations showing the Old Time Gospel Hour, and a total ministry income of in excess of sixty million dollars annually. He has indeed come a long way! We will have more to say about Rev. Falwell in Chapter Six when we discuss televangelism and politics in America.

The Rev. Jim Bakker

Jim Bakker traces the "birth" of the PTL (Praise The Lord or People That Love) Network to January, 1974, in Charlotte, N.C., just over ten years ago. While PTL was born in adversity in Charlotte, Bakker himself was born in Muskegon Heights, Michigan, to a family that would easily fit the profile of Mass Media Members developed in Chapter Three. At some point, of course, Bakker was

99

JIM BAKKER

"born again."

Our research indicates that his family was emersed in the Assemblies of God faith, and was typically devout. However, it seems that the young Jim Bakker did not "cotton" all that much to the family religion. Although he speaks in generalities about it, Bakker reports that he found himself in considerable difficulty in his local church because he was a "rock-n-roll" disc jockey. Apparently, an Elder of the church stood-up for him at the height of the difficulty and it was satisfactorily resolved. Hadden and Swann report that the young Jim Bakker had the misfortune of running over a young child, and the accident served as a precipitating event in turning Bakker back to the religion of his parents.1 Although the child Bakker ran over did recover, the effect of the event was to have profound implications for Bakker. One outcome was that he entered North Central Bible College to study for the ministry. Although Bakker did not graduate from Bible College, he was, nevertheless, ordained. In 1983, North Central Bible College announced, on the Bakker program, that the college would award Bakker an honorary doctorate. The honorary doctorate of divinity degree was awarded in ceremonies held in May, at the North Central Bible commencement for 1984.

According to Bakker, he and Tammy had begun their ministry in Minneapolis, 19 years before the founding of the PTL Television Network. Bakker indicates that he was, for a while, a travelling evangelist, earning only meager sums of money. Apparently, his first major ministry was with Pat Robertson's Christian Broadcasting Network (CBN), where Jim and Pat co-hosted a religious talk show and Jim, along with Tammy Faye, did a children's puppet show. The Bakker's were at CBN for a little less than eight years, at which time Jim "received God's direction to give his resignation."2 Bakker insists that he and Pat Robertson parted company on friendly terms. It is instructive, however, that one can watch Robertson's 700 Club hour after hour, and if Bakker's name has ever been mentioned, we clearly missed it. The obverse, however, is not true-- Jim often mentions Pat Robertson by name on the PTL Club Show. Whether Jim left CBN on friendly terms with Pat Robertson is unimportant-- he did leave. In fact, he left to go to sunny Southern California to work with Paul Crouch in establishing the "Trinity Broadcasting Network." According to Bakker:3

> We had gone there to do what I thought was
> going to be my life's work for God. .... We
> settled in, bought a home. I thought that
> finally after 11 years of ministering I was
> going to have a ministry of my own. But
> through a series of events, the door was
> closed..."

The "series of events" that "closed" the door was a
falling-out between Bakker and Crouch, an event which
led to Jim's "decision" to leave the confines of
Southern California.

The Bakker's departed California for North Carolina,
and after arriving in Charlotte, Jim began the PTL
Network in an empty furniture store in that city. From
"a staff of six...a modified furniture store
studio...[and] one television affiliate," PTL has grown
to the multi-million dollar enterprise it is today.4

The road to acquiring the "1,360 acres of rolling
hills, tall pines and small, peaceful lakes" just
outside of Charlotte has not, however, always been
smooth for the Bakkers.5 On January 2, 1978, Jim and
PTL broke ground for the building of Heritage USA. That
event put in motion a series of continuing financial
crises that have sent Jim to his PTL television
partners, teary eyed, again and again. Each time he has
asked for money, more money, and then more money.The
financial crises never seem to end at PTL. For example,
in 1979 the evangelical publication "Christianity
Today" reported that PTL was "in danger of going
under."6 According to "Christianity Today," PTL had
amassed over $13 million in debts, and approximately $6
million of its monthly accounts were past due.7 What
did Bakker do? He did what he always does, he went on
the PTL Network and pleaded with his viewers for
"immediate help." In fact, Bakker's financial crisis
was so "immediate" that he appealed for people to use
their credit cards to make their pledges so that Bakker
could get the cash more quickly. Christianity Today
characterized PTL as "Please Toss a Lifesaver," and
reported that "some station managers have expressed
displeasure over Bakker's increasingly high-pressure
appeals for funds, and one accused him of
`manipulating' unwary donors with misleading
statements."8 There simply never seemed, and still
never seems, to be enough money. Even today, Jim looks

out at his audience with his earnest, glowing smile and tells his viewers that they must send in their pledges or PTL will be taken off the air by many television stations.

According to Bakker, he was investigated by several agencies of the Federal Government over a number of years.For example, Bakker had considerable difficulty with the Federal Communications Commission (FCC). What lead to the scrap with the FCC was a report in The Charlotte Observer alleging that Bakker had diverted hundereds of thousands of dollars from accounts with money raised for overseas ministries to accounts used to pay current bills and to pay for domestic projects.9 To do so, of course, is a violation of law. As Christianity Today reported, the Charlotte Observer's information was based "upon PTL documents and interviews with former PTL executives and overseas Christian leaders."10 As a result of these revelations, and donor complaints, the FCC sent two investigators down to Charlotte to look into the matter. Bakker did not cooperate with the FCC investigators, however, and vowed to do combat with the FCC in court. However, Bakker did promise that we would eventually fulfil the diverted pledges. If the reader desires to learn the outcome of this particular PTL crisis, we invite the reader to watch the Bakker program a few times-- Jim usually doesn't go very long without triumphantly bringing the outcome to the awareness of his viewers. As Bakker proudly tells it, the Feds came at him in every possible way, and could find nothing wrong. Bakker believes that he went against the might of the Federal bureaucracy and came away unscathed. He delights in telling how those people who have tried to "get him" have lost their jobs, gone bankrupt, and even moved out of the United States. The viewer is left with impression that God has severely punished those persons who have dared to mess with Jim Bakker. In light of this, we find it interesting that Bakker constantly refers to Isaiah 54:17, which says that "no weapon formed against you shall prosper."

Bakker is not a big man; in fact, he is noticeably small in stature. In a recent telethon to raise money for PTL's $30 million dollar hotel, Jim offered a reproduction of the Yaacov Heller statute of little David slaying Golaith. On the base of the statute he had inscribed the quote from Isaiah, mentioned above. Perhaps Jim Bakker-- fresh from battles with the

Federal bureaucracy, the City of Charlotte, and other co-horts of the devil who have "come against" him-- views himself as a "David" in today's secular world. In a recent PTL Partner letter received by one of the authors, Bakker seemed to confirm this idea:

> Tammy and I have an unusual thing that we like to do. When we sit and look at our David and Goliath sculpture, we like to place different names on the old giant lying there. It helps us think back on all the victories that God has won for us. And the story of David and Goliath gives us great faith for the future victories we are going to have when we continue to go forth in His name, unafraid of of the giants in the land.

Whether or not he has actually "slain some giants" along the way, Bakker seems, at a minimum, to have succeeded in building his own multi-million dollar bureaucracy composed of the PTL Sattelite Network, Heritage Village, Heritage USA, and numerous other facilities, against rather large odds. On the June 1st telecast of the Jim Bakker show, Rev. Bakker said that Heritage USA had recently been appraised. What was the appraised value?-- 77 million dollars! In fact, Bakker's PTL Club Show was asked to help open the World's Fair in New Orleans during the Summer of 1984. Not bad for a small, retiring fellow from Muskegon Heights, Michigan!

If one visits Heritage USA, one is greeted by mostly young, energetic, rosy-cheeked men and women who, at the drop of a hat, are quick to say "Praise the Lord!" or "Glory to God!" It is almost impossible to talk with one of the lower level employees for very long without hearing their personal testimonial or having them "witness." One is constantly reassured, unsolicited, of the wonderfulness of Jim and Tammy Bakker. During a visit to the "Upper Room" we were told by the pastor on duty that Heritage USA was "not another Jonestown"; a thought that had not occured to us but, nevertheless, is an interesting comparison. It is difficult not to be cynical and believe that one is experiencing "contrived" happiness while at Heritage USA. However, contrived or not, it seems to "rub off" on most of the visitors to the PTL facility.

When one begins to get closer to the upper

administrative positions of PTL, however, the mood of the employees seems to become more somber. They are less willing to talk about PTL. In fact, they will make promises with no intention of keeping them. One of PTL's senior executive officers even claimed to have returned telephone calls when, in fact, he had not.After three weeks of disclaimers, the vice-president in question did finally call. It seems that when someone gets close to the top of PTL there is a kind of "circle the wagons" mentality in which claiming to have done things that were not done, is acceptable. The closer one gets, the more somber the reactions become, and the glowing testimonials tend to disappear.

The Rev. Jimmy Swaggart

The Reverend Jimmy Swaggart evokes some strong emotions and criticism from many corners of American society. He is also able to attract very large groups of people to his crusades. Some of the statements he makes in his fiery, and emotional preaching turn a lot of people off, but Jimmy doesn't mind. Before he makes a controversial remark he often says, "Now I know a lot of you are not going to like this but I don't care, I work for God and he told me to say this." The following are just a few of his more interesting statements: "We have trouble with abortion, pronography, and violence in the United States because the pulpits have been silent"; "The World and National Council of Churches work for the Devil. If you go to a church which supports these councils, get out! I'm talking about the Episcopal, United Methodists, Presbyterian, and Lutherans."

A favorite list of topics in Swaggart's sermons include, beside those already mentioned, homosexuals, Marxism and communism in the world, secular humanism in America, apostacy in the pulpits of America and the mainline churches, socialism, busing for racial equality, E.R.A., liberal politicians, the United States Supreme Court, and parents who set bad examples for their children. The list could go on. Most important, however, is the fact that Swaggart preaches on the topics in a very convincing and dramatic manner.

105

JIMMY
SWAGGART

A Swaggart service in a crusade (some would say show), begins with Jimmy playing the piano and singing some gospel songs. He plays the piano well and has a good voice. He comes from the same musical background that produced Jerry Lee Lewis and Mickey Gilley, both cousins of Jimmy Swaggart. After the music comes the sermon. Swaggart paces back and forth on the stage with his Bible held aloft, expounding on the evils of America and God's answer from His Holy Word. He sweats profusely at times, often removing his glasses and drying his face while making a point. He knows the methods of effective sermon delivery. He gets right into his subject once his message begins. It is not uncommon for the audience to give him a standing ovation when he makes a very controversial statement. A lot of people who attend his crusades seem to strongly approve of such statements. We have observed him speaking in tongues in the middle of a sermon. People in the audience sometimes break out in tongue-speaking, and when they do, Jimmy stops preaching and waits until they are done. The services are very emotional and, Jimmy would say, spirit filled. Many come down to be saved, healed, and filled with the Holy Spirit. As with the other T.V. preachers, the content of Reverend Swaggart's sermons always include a call to repentance and to be "born again."

Like Jim Bakker, Jimmy Swaggart is a builder. He is currently finishing the construction of the "Jimmy Swaggart Bible College" in Baton Rouge, Louisiana. Plans are to open the college for its first class of students in the Fall of 1984. Swaggart is also building a new church building at his headquarters in Baton Rouge. In addition to his domestic building programs, Jimmy is building churches and schools in a number of different countries. He is also involved in feeding children at various spots around the world. Of course, all of these activities cost money, and Swaggart, like Jim Bakker, is constantly pleading for money from his viewers and supporters. Swaggart gets in front of the television cameras and opines that "it really pains me" to continually ask for money. But ask, and ask, and ask he must; and, ask, and ask, and ask, he does.

The Jimmy Swaggart Evangelist Association is not without controversy. Perhaps he brings most of it on himself with his constant triads against different religious groups, social and political institutions. One thing is certain, his constant frontal attacks on what he perceives as "enemies of the Body of Christ," have gotten him some bad publicity in the popular press and resulted in at least two television stations cancelling the telecast of his crusades.

Swaggart's wife has been criticized (on a PBS Television Special on the Jimmy Swaggart ministry) for purhcasing an office desk valued at $11,000. He has also been cast in a bad light when it was reveaded that he "borrowed" several hundred thousand dollars fron the Jimmy Swaggart Evangelistic Association to purchase property and build two large houses for himself and his son. However, Swaggart claims to be the first T.V. preacher to provide an audited financial disclosure statement for anyone who cares to ask for one.

Controversial he may be, but Jimmy Lee Swaggart is, nevertheless, one powerful evangelical preacher. As far as we can tell, Swaggart has no real intentions of backing off of his fundamentalist, evangelical message and, we would suggest, hundred of thousands of people in America will continue to flock to hear his crusades.

The Rev. Pat Robertson

Every group of people has its intellectual leader, a person who seems to be brighter, quicker, and more intelligent than his or her colleagues. The Mass Media Ministers, being mortal humans, are no exception. Among the T.V. preachers, the resident intellectual is, in our opinion, Marion G. "Pat" Robertson of the Christian Broadcasting Network (CBN). As one looks at the educational attainment of the bulk of the "Bright Stars" of Christian television-- Jim Bakker, Oral Roberts, Jimmy Swaggart, one finds that most of them are not well educated. Robertson, on the other hand, has outstanding educational credentials. He is a Phi Beta Kappa graduate of Washington and Lee University, and a graduate of Yale University Law School. Robertson was Commissioned as an Officer of Marines, obtaining the rank of Captain and serving the United States in Korea. He has also been a businessman, working in electronic components. If one investigates the success of CBN, it seems clear that he has learned the lessons of business very well.

108

PAT
ROBERTSON

Robertson worked out a deal to purchase a UHF television station in Virginia Beach, Virginia. As Hadden and Swann report, buying the T.V. station was itself somewhat of a "miracle," because Pat really had no money with which to close the deal.[11] Apparently, he made his way financially by preaching in various Virginia churches, finally securing enough money "to put the station back on the air in October 1, 1961."[12] Pat Robertson is a handsome man with a pleasant presentation of self. He is of average build with graying hair in the right places to give him a rather distinguished look. In keeping with his educational attainment, he has a very good command of spoken English. Although he does not come off as an intellectual, one feels certain that he is a knowledgable and thorough person. Robertson's knowledge and grasp of world problems and events is impressive. He gives every appearance of being honestly concerned about human problems in the world. Overlaying all of his personal qualities is the fact that Robertson seems to be a first-rate preacher. Jimmy Swaggart is, as we have suggested, also an excellent preacher; but Pat Robertson's style and presentation is clearly different than Swaggart's. Unlike Swaggart's hell-fire and brimstone tirads against wickedness in America and the world, Robertson is a particularly up-beat preacher. He seems to always be smiling, laughing, and praising the Lord with gladness. His positiveness does not, it seems to us, suggest a flippant attitude about world events and circumstances; rather, in our opinion, Robertson sees events and circumstances as the work of the Lord, and he views himself as a man of God. One does not come to the end of a telecast of the 700 Club Show feeling depressed and remorseful. Quite the contrary is true!

The "700 Club" is Pat Robertson's regular telecast on CBN, being aired daily and lasting for 90 minutes. The show is much like a variety/magazine show one might see on secular television. Guests come and go through short, pointed interviews, in which the constant theme of salvation through Jesus Christ is presented to the viewer. Music is sometimes a part of the show as well. Quite often a special report on some troubled aspect of the world will be presented by a CBN employee who is on the scene.

Pat often gives brief sermonettes on what he calls the "Kingdom Principles" of God. The basic message is "give and you shall receive," and the more you give to

God (the work of God), the more you can expect to receive. Robertson makes it clear that he believe's that one of the best ways to accomplish the working of the "Kingdom Principles" is to give to the 700 Club.

As with most of the religious programs on television, a main component of the 700 Club is the message of redemption and salvation. Prayer too is a major portion of the presentation. Pat and his co-hosts often pray for healing-- physical, spiritual, and financial. Robertson prays for specific ailments (not persons), which he is apparently instructed to do through "Words of Knowledge" given him by the Holy Spirit. It seems that these "Words of Knowledge" can be presented to Robertson at any time, even as he is praying out loud. On one occasion when we were watching the 700 Club, Pat prayed and announced that warts and moles were falling off of people all over America.

Unlike Jim Bakker's PTL Satellite Network, Robertson's CBN does not telecast exclusively religious programming. In addition to the 700 Club and other T.V. preachers who are seen on CBN, the network runs a number of old movies, and western and comedy series. Such shows as Groucho Marks' "You Bet Your Life," "Leave it to Beaver," "The Rifleman," and others, can be seen regularly on CBN. Pat is also producing his own "Christian Soaps" for telecast on CBN. Robertson aims for CBN to become a fourth commercial network in America.

On Robertson's 700 Club Show, the basic message of Christian fundamentalism is not sacrificed. The five basic tenets of Christian fundamentalism mentioned earlier are at the heart of the presentation. What seems to be strikingly different is that the image projected by Pat and his co-hosts is clearly more middle-class than other T.V. preachers. One is impressed with the fact that, unlike Jim Bakker, Jimmy Swaggart, Oral Roberts and others, Pat Robertson seldom makes grammatical errors as he speaks. Nor, for that matter, do his co-hosts. Robertson seems to be appealing to modern, mainstream America.

The Rev. Robert Schuller

The Reverend Robert Schuller has a smile which can

111

sparkle off the glass walls of his Crystal Cathedral. He begins his church service by coming to the pulpit dressed in very impressive, priestly attire; wearing a robe, a medallion, and using hand gestures which conjure images of the high priest about to enter the Holy of Holies before the Lord. It does not take a great stretch of the imagination, as one watches his church services, to recognize that Schuller tries to convey, and perhaps feels the presence of God in the Crystal Cathedral. The Reverend Schuller is ordained in the Reformed Church in America. He has been perfecting his style as a televangelist over the last 14 years, and he has developed a style that is clearly unique among the current "bright stars" of Christian television. His religious broadcast is called the "Hour of Power" and originates from the Crystal Cathedral located in Garden Grove, California. The Cathedral is a huge glass structure with over 10,000 glass windows. It was built, in part, by "selling" 10,000 of its windows to believers for $500 apiece. It is estimated that the Crystal Cathedral is a $20 million glass-and-steel latticework structure. The Wall Street Journal claims that Schuller reaches 2.7 million viewers who are tuned in to his "Hour of Power" telecast on 190 television stations around the United States.

Many of Reverend Schuller's sermons are closely tied to the power of positive thinking philosophy of Norman Vincent Peale. His sermons are usually about God wanting his people to concentrate on the positive aspects of life and the gospel. As he approaches the pulpit he says, with hands uplifted, "this is a day which the Lord has made, let us rejoice and be glad in it! Throughout his sermons Reverend Schuller will voice several slogans which reinforce what he calls "possibility thinking." Some examples are: "You'll never advance until you take a chance"; "God never starts a project and abandons it! God is no quitter. He is a finisher!"; "Yes, faith is a noun-- but it must become a verb! Action!."

After the preliminaries, he begins his sermon, always with a positive note. While Reverend Schuller stresses the good in being a follower of Christ, he does not entirely neglect the negative, sinful nature which can be seen in mankind. But in his well constructed sermons, even the recognition of a negative, sinful nature comes out as a call to enter the glorious Kingdom of God. One can easily come away from one of

ROBERT
SCHULLER

his services feeling that he has seen a pastor that not only ministers to his flock, but one who also calls sinners, in a gentle way, to repentance and the "born again" experience. That the content and method of delivery of his sermons is reaching many people is evidenced by the numbers who are packed into the Crystal Cathedral and those seated in their cars in the adjacent drive-in sanctuary. Robert Schuller is telecast on many television stations and on Bakker's PTL Satellite Network. Of course, station and satellite time does cost money. However, the Reverend Schuller's ministry, and the appeal of his preaching, have success built into them.

When Reverend Schuller preaches he is fond of talking about the Crystal Cathedral and how it came to be built by faith. He also stresses that his ministry expends far less money for each person it reaches than is spent by the smaller, mainline churches on each person they reach in their ministries. This means, according to Robert Schuller, that his ministry from the Crystal Cathedral is much more cost-effective than many smaller, less effecient churches.

In recent months, what Schuller calls "America's most-watched church service" has included a new twist: its pastor's constant references to his new books. In the May 3rd issue of the Wall Street Journal, Paula Span reported that:13

> On next Sunday's broadcast, Jeff Keith, a college athlete planning a cross-country run despite a leg lost to cancer, tells how a letter from his grandmother restored his flagging confidence with a page torn, literally, from Mr. Schuller's latest best seller. Thereupon, Mr. Schuller hands young Mr. Keith a copy of "Tough-Minded Faith for Tenderhearted People" and invites him to read aloud the rousing self-exhortations: "God never starts a project and abandons it! God is no quitter. He is a finisher!" If this is a typical week, enough viewers and others will buy either "Tough-Minded Faith" (with more than 300,000 copies in print since December) or its even more popular forerunner "Tough Times Never Last but Tough People Do!" (about 420,000 in print) to keep both titles riding the New York Times best-seller list.

Apparently, Reverend Schuller's books have become
such best-sellers that he has taken to promoting them
on his "Hour of Power" program. As Paula Span went on
to report, the Christian Booksellers Association annual
survey clearly documents the excellent health of
religious bookstores. She reports that their sales rose
15.9 percent last year and that sales even grew a
respectable 5.5 percent during the recent recession.14
However, the publisher of Schuller's books (Thomas
Nelson publishers of Nashville), "estimates that
two-thirds of Mr. Schuller's sales are coming from the
secular market, not the nation's 6,000 to 8,000
religious bookstores."15 His books have sold so well,
and Rev. Schuller is becoming so well known, that he
was the guest on Cable News Network's (CNN) "Newsmaker
Sunday" program on May 20, 1984. The narrator felt some
need to justify having a preacher on a newsmaker
program, and he opened the telecast by stating that
never before has a minister of the Gospel had two
titles on the best seller list at the same time. It
seems that Reverend Schuller is not only a "bright
star" of Christian television, but he is fast becoming
a noted author on the secular American scene, as well.

In this chapter we have outlined and discussed the
basic elements of the Christian,
evangelical-fundamentalist position in the United
States. We have also tried to illustrate that the
"bright stars" of modern-day Christian television could
not have attained the heights they currently enjoy had
it not been for the pioneering work of the "guiding
lights"-- Billy Graham, Rex Humbard, and Oral Roberts.
Provide the way the "guiding lights" did, however, and
their early efforts gave birth to the "bright stars"--
the Jerry Falwells, Jim Bakkers, Jimmy Swaggarts, Pat
Robertsons, and Robert Schuller's of today. The "bright
stars" have taken Christian television farther, we are
sure, than Graham, Roberts, and Humbard ever dreamed.
In fact, the "bright stars" have spawned a number of
aspiring young stars of Christian television we call
the "rising stars." In addition to those T.V. preachers
we call the "rising stars," the "bright stars" have
made it possible for a number of different kinds of
Christian T.V. shows to find their way to the T.V.
tube. In Chapter Five we will discuss the "rising
stars" and many of the musical, variety, and bible
prophecy shows now available to the viewer of Christian
television.

PREACHING TO ALL NATIONS: RISING STARS, BIBLE
PROPHECY, AND CHRISTIAN VARIETY

PREACHING TO ALL NATIONS: RISING STARS, BIBLE PROPHECY,
AND CHRISTIAN VARIETY

INTRODUCTION

For I say unto you, Among those that are
born of women there is not a greater prophet
than John the Baptist: but he that is least in
the kingdom of God is greater than he.

Luke 7:28

In the first four chapters of this book we have
concentrated on those T.V. preachers who are "lights
unto nations"-- Jim Bakker, Rex Humbard, Jerry Falwell,
Oral Roberts, Pat Robertson, and Jimmy Lee Swaggart.
These men are, in our opinion, "guiding lights" and
"bright stars" by virtue of their national and
international television ministries. In this chapter we
will pause and look at those T.V. preachers who are
struggling in the vineyards, patiently (perhaps)
awaiting their own rise to stardom among the Mass Media

119

Ministers. We have in mind, and will introduce the
reader to, television ministers such as Jerry Savelle,
Kenneth Copeland, Bob Tilton, and James Robison.

As Hadden and Swann pointed-out in their recent book,
Prime Time Preachers, the three religious networks are
already crowded with television evangelists. The
several preachers we named as struggling in the
vineyards seem, to us, to be the most likely candidates
for experiencing a rise to prime time stardom. No one
knows, however, how many folks are out there-- praying,
preparing, and perhaps plotting to make an entrance
into religious television. Like becoming a Hollywood
star, however, the probability of an unknown "making
it" on religious television is rather remote without a
sponsor-- not impossible, but remote. It seems
reasonable that if one is going to purchase air-time
from CBN or PTL, one must be acceptable to Pat
Robertson or Jim Bakker. In fact, PTL began 1984 with a
series of new programs produced by Jim Bakker. We are
impressed, as we watch these new programs, with the
homage that is paid to Jim Bakker, the PTL Network,
and, occasionally to Tammy Bakker. We do not know if
the "stars" of these shows must praise and compliment
Bakker and the PTL Network; we suspect, however, that
shows that were critical would not be long tolerated.

Like everyone else, the T.V. ministers are mortal
men, and like most people, they do not desire to see
their life's work end with their death. It seems
reasonable, therefore, that the Mass Media Ministers
would make provisions for their ministries to carry-on
after they have departed this life. Perhaps they recall
the story of Eli'jah and Eli'sha as told in Second
Kings of the Old Testament, and therefore, a few
examples of biblical bases for "passing the mantle" may
be instructive.

ON PASSING THE MANTLE

In the Gospel according to St. Luke, we read of the
transfiguration of Jesus on a mountain (Lk. 9:28-36).
There Jesus, along with his disciples, Peter, John, and
James, prayed. According to the Gospel story, Jesus was
met by, and interacted with, Moses and Elijah. The

120

witnessing of this event so moved Peter that he wanted
to build a tabernacle to commerate what he had seen.
The Biblical significance of this event seems to be
that Jesus fulfills the promise of both the Law (Moses)
and The Prophets (Elijah).

In the Old Testament book of Exodus, we see that
Moses, after his long leadership of the children of
Israel, passed his leadership on to Joshua, who led
Israel into the promised land. While Moses was given a
vision of the promised land, he had to pass on the
actual carrying out of the promise to Joshua.

Also in the Old Testament we find Elijah passing on
his lifes work. Elijah became, in the tradition of the
Hebrew religion, the model of a prophet of God. Elijah
waged a long and bitter battle with the King of Israel,
and with his wife Jezebel, over the issue of idolatry,
which Elijah saw happening as a result of the growing
worship of Baal. In his tumultuous career, Elijah not
only faced danger,he preached, healed, and prepared a
protege'. The person he taught, trained, and encouraged
(his protege') was named Elisha. In the Old Testament
story (2 Kings, Chapter 2), Elijah had to move on. The
Bible story says that he went up into the heavens in a
chariot of fire. Just as he was caught up, he passed
his mantle on to Elisha who carried on his total
ministry.

Like the prophets of old, the television preachers
obviously see themselves as carrying on this ancient
tradition. When we watch the T.V. church, we see
bright, promising young preachers given the chance to
present their interpretation of the Gospel on the
satellite networks. Men like Jim Bakker, Oral Roberts,
and Jimmy Swaggart, view themselves as preparing, like
Elijah, to pass on their mantle.

THE RISING STARS

Let no man despise thy youth; but be thou an
example of the believers, in word, in conversation,
in charity, in spirit, in faith, in purity.
Till I come, give attendance to reading, to

121

exhortation, to doctrine.
Neglect not the gift that is in thee, which was
given thee by prophecy, with the laying on of the
hands of the presbytery.

I Timothy 4:12-14

The Rev. Bob Tilton: The "Word of Faith"

   Bob Tilton is a handsome man. He has a full head of
brown hair, eyes that are set well apart, and a big,
inviting smile. His wife, Marte, is as attractive as
Bob is handsome. Together they present a picture of a
well groomed, articulate, and prosperous American
couple. Bob Tilton has a number of different
"ministries" to which he attends. His "Word of Faith"
ministries include his "Word of Faith" service
broadcast live on the PTL Network and many metro T.V.
and local cable systems. Tilton also administers
various construction projects for his Dallas based
operations-- a Garden Learning Center is nearing
completion, and Tilton has announced plans for a Garden
Television Center. The T.V. center will be a 33-foot
tall, 19,500 square-foot building designed to house
Word of Faith's expanding television and communications
facilities. Tilton's "Word of Faith World Outreach
Center" contracts with other churches to hook-up with
Pastor Tilton to receive Christian programming via
satellite. In a recent issue of the "Times Arrow," a
tabloid published by the Tilton ministries, Bob
stated:1

          WE'RE 1,100 STRONG ... AND STILL GROWING!!!
          The Word of Faith Satellite Ministry in only
          one year's time has surpassed the 1,000 mark!
          Over 1,000 affiliate churches are hooking in
          each month to receive live messages via
          satellite from top notch speakers like
          Charles Capps, Marilyn Hickey, Novel Hayes
          and T.L. Osborn as well as monthly concerts
          with such gospel greats as The Imperials,
          Phil Driscoll, Silverwind, and Phil Keaggy.
          You too can become a vital part of this
          growing network.

   Reverend Bob Tilton also has a "ministry" which he

BOB TILTON

calls the "Success-n-Life" program. By this he means that with his guidance and supporting materials (which he will send for a small donation to his ministry), he can guarantee that you will reap the rewards of success. It is Pastor Tilton's apparent contention that he knows the secret of the success which God wants for every person. On his regular teaching show, which can be seen on the PTL Satellite Network, he constantly refers to the same theme, no matter what his expressed message for the day happens to be. If he begins with Bible exposition, the talk ends with a statement on giving money. If he begins with the "born again" experience, he still ends with a discussion about giving money.

Tilton makes it plain that his church is a "full gospel church." During his regular Sunday service he preaches a sermon which hits heavily, once again, on giving money to his ministry. We recently saw one of his services in which he said, "Now I want you to get out your Bibles, and also your checkbooks." The people in the congregation dutifully opened their Bibles, and we observed many opening their checkbooks as well. We would hasten to remind the reader than in the Methodist, Catholic, Episcopal, Baptist, or other more traditional churches, there is an appointed time in the service to worship the Lord with tithes and offerings. In the traditional, mainline churches one does not hear the continual, impassioned pleas and direct orders to give to the ministry of the individual pastor.

To the uninitiated, a Bob Tilton service can be a little unsettling, and, perhaps, even abrasive. We have heard some people compare Bob with a slick "insurance" or "used car" salesman. Some folks, from a more traditional religious tradition, get upset by Bob's approach to worshipping the Lord with continual appeals for money and more money. Others that we have talked to have said that Tilton's methods are tantamount to commercialization of the Gospel message and negate the beauty of singing the Doxology during the presentation of the tithes and offerings. The reader will have to decide this issue for him or her self.

The Reverend Tilton and his wife Marte have other talents. We watched his service recently and saw, somewhat to our amazement, Bob and the congregation singing and speaking in tongues. Although it may happen elsewhere, we have never seen any person-- let alone an entire congregation, singing in tongues. In this particular service, many, if not most in the congregation were enjoying the serivce by clapping their hands, jumping, dancing, and raising their hands to the Lord. Also during this service, Marte Tilton read from the constitution of the United States and made appropriate remarks about applying the constitution to Christianity in America. She reminded the congregation and viewers on television that she and Bob are the hosts for the National Day of Prayer celebration at Constitutional Hall in Washington, D.C., on May 3rd. This event is telecast on CBN, PTL, TBN, and other local stations. There is, of course, a potential audience of millions across America and the rest of the world. Bob Tilton is indeed one of the "rising stars" whose brilliance is increasing.

The Rev. Kenneth Copeland: The "Believer's Voice of Victory"

Kenneth Copeland is not a handsome man in the same sense that Bob Tilton is handsome. Not that Copeland is unattractive, he isn't. What Kenneth Copeland is, is tall; in fact, he is tall and gangly with a pronounced saunter in his gate. Kenneth's wife Gloria is, on the other hand, a very attractive lady who presents a well tailored look. She seems to be aware of her presentation of self, showing good posture without the obvious effort that those unaccustomed to it often evidence.

If Kenneth Copeland is anything, he is a first-rate preacher who enjoys teaching and fostering the gospel message. He is, in addition, a fun preacher to hear and to watch. It seems that once Copeland opens his mouth, his arms and feet must also go into motion. As far as we can tell, Reverend Copeland cannot teach the gospel in a low key, conventional way. Once he starts preaching he leaves the pulpit and walks among the audience. His sermons are punctuated with interesting, personal vignettes concerning such things as going fishing as a young boy and cutting the grass, or settling estates and standing by deeds of trust. His audience seems to enjoy his preaching as much as Reverend Copeland enjoys doing it; the audience often can be seen laughing, and waving their hands in praise to the Lord.

125

KENNETH
COPELAND

While Copeland clearly enjoys teaching and preaching the gospel message, he never departs from the five basic tenets of Christian fundamentalism discussed in Chapter Four. As Copeland walks among his audience he will often shout "Glory to God, Glory to God..... Glory, Glory, Glory...... Glory to God!" His message is basic: repent and ask forgiveness, accept Jesus as your personal savior and be "born again," be filled with the Holy Spirit, and your life will take a dramatic turn for the better.

Like other T.V. preachers, Kenneth Copeland's "Believers' Voice of Victory" program emphasizes all of the various ministries, including healing. His most enduring message, however, is to "get into the Word of God"-- learn it, believe it, know it, internalize it, and begin to practice it. Once the Word of God has been internalized into your spirit (Copeland often places both hands onto his lower chest area for emphasis), the Word will act as an agent of control in the believers life. This is not something Copeland just preaches, he believes in it!

In talking about Kenneth Copeland, it is also necessary to talk about his wife, Gloria. We have already commented that she is an attractive, well groomed person. Beyond that, Mrs. Copeland is also a fine preacher as well. She is often featured on her husband's televised crusades. While her mannerisms are more reserved than are Kenneth's, her message is basically the same. It is communicated very effectively. She is as much an asset to her husband as Marte Tilton is to Bob Tilton; perhaps, in fact, she is more of an asset.

Copeland's T.V. shows end with Kenneth and Gloria on camera with an empty, or emptying arena in the background. Mrs. Copeland usually reminds viewers that it is important for them to be where the Spirit is, and encourages people to come to their crusades because the Holy Spirit is always present during a Copeland crusade. Reverend Copeland then prays for the people and encourages them to keep learning and to get into the Word of God. The telecast ends with with the offering of tapes as premium gifts as an inducement for financial contributions to the Ft. Worth based Copeland ministries. We have never seen the Copeland's weep about their financial plight or plead for money to save their financially troubled ministry. They usually offer the tapes, suggesting that they will be a "blessing" to those who send for them.

We enjoy watching the Copelands. Kenneth is not only a well prepared and powerful preacher, he is also entertaining and fun to watch. He is, in our opinion, a "rising star" on the verge of becoming a "bright star."

The Rev. Jerry Savelle: "Adventures in Faith"

Jerry Savelle is, as far as we can tell, a disciple of Kenneth Copeland. While Copeland is tall, Savelle is not. He is, however, an attractive, well groomed man with a small, neatly trimmed mustache. Reverend Savelle is married, with an attractive wife (Carolyn) and two attractive teenage daughters (Jerrianne and Terri). His Fort-Worth based television ministry, entitled "Adventures in Faith," is broadcast on Monday nights on the PTL Satellite Network, and 13 other T.V. stations from Florida to South Dakota.

Reverend Savelle's preaching style is much like Kenneth Copeland's, but not quite as effective in the humor department. Jerry's voice, compared to most preachers we have heard, is high pitched and sometimes a little shrill. He nevertheless preaches some interesting, and often entertaining sermons. We have heard him preach on such topics as "Wake up the Mighty Men," "Take the City," "Where are the Elijahs of God," and others.

Like Kenneth Copeland, Jerry Savelle frequently leaves the puplit and walks down among his audience while he is preaching. If he makes an important point and the audience doesn't respond, he will turn his head toward them and with an inquiring look say "Hello? Are you there?" The audience usually responds by laughing, clapping their hands, or saying Amen.

In one broadcast of "Adventures in Faith," Savelle called people to the front for them to be filled with the Holy Spirit and to receive the "gift of tongues." Many people came down and prayed a prayer with Reverend Savelle. When Saveile ended the prayer by saying "receive the Holy Spirit," many folks held their hands into the air and began speaking in unknown tongues. One

128

particular gentleman appeared to be having some difficulty in acquiring his own unknown language, so Savelle attended to him personally, laying on his hands and speaking in tongues himself, exhorting the man to let loose and let the Spirit speak through him. Because everyone around the gentleman was already speaking in tongues, we could not tell if he ever received "the gift."

Like the Copelands, Savelle ends his "Adventures in Faith" show by offering tapes or "mini-books" in exchange for financial contributions to his ministry. Jerry Savelle is clearly a "rising star." This status is reflected in his apparent deference to Copeland and in the sophistication of his mass mailings. While Savelle is on PTL, his show is only 30 minutes in duration. We would characterize Jerry Savelle as a "twinkling star"-- not one of the brilliant "rising stars," but clearly a T.V. preacher whose light is getting brighter.

The Rev. James Robison: "In The Word"

James Robison is a large man with a full head of thick, dark hair. He is difficult to ignore when he preaches in the charasmatic style that he has. However, in spite of his size and vigorous presentation of the gospel mesage, he has a voice that is, at times, soft and even gentle. He can also thunder like a prophet when he chooses to do so. In keeping with the more gentle side of his preaching, he is not ashamed to weep in the public pulpit. When he does cry, he gives every appearance of being a man who is deeply touched by the plight of the people who are "lost" and suffering from their own sin and the sins of the church and society. Robison talks a great deal about the sin he has uncovered in his own life and how he had to ask God's forgiveness for being arrogant, pround, and for saying "bad things" about other T.V. preachers. There was a time in Robison's ministry when he openly criticized and "made fun" of folks like Jim Bakker and Kenneth Copeland. In the context of what he calls his own spiritual enlightment, Robison reports travelling around the country visiting such personalities as Oral Roberts, Jim and Tammy Bakker, Kenneth Copeland, and others to ask for their forgiveness for his unabashed criticism of them. We witnessed Reverend Robison making

JAMES ROBINSON

a public confession to Jim Bakker and his wife Tammy. James Robison gave every public evidence of being very contrite.

In his sermons he hammers away on the theme of the "new birth" just as the other T.V. preachers. One of his newest and most recent themes, however, is the coming together in unity of the "Body of Christ." This seems to be somewhat of a modification of the message we heard him preaching only a few months ago. Then he talked a good bit about the apostacy in the mainline churches and in the pulpits of those churches. While he has not stopped saying those sort of things entirely, there has been a shift of emphasis in his sermons. His sermons now include much more material on the subject of the need for the T.V. preachers to join together to do battle with the forces of evil in American society. He seems particularly interested in saying that he supports the ministry and building projects of Jim Bakker of PTL fame. During one segment of the Jim Bakker Show, Robison said, "brother if I can help in your project I will even push a wheel-barrow."

When viewing Reverend Robison it is difficult for one to maintain a stance of objectivity and resist being caught up in the spirit of the moment. He is very effective in his sermon delivery. His sermon content is basic, evangelical Christianity: the Son of God, the need for forgiveness, the "born again" experience, becoming a follower of Christ, and being an active Christian in the affairs of the world. As previously mentioned, he delivers the sermon in a very emotional way, with a profusion of Bible quotations, and with a very convincing presentation of himself. He is one of the brighter "rising stars" of the television church.

CHRISTIAN VARIETY PROGRAMMING

When he ascended up on high, he led
captivity captive, and gave gifts unto men. (Now
that he ascended, what is it but that he also
decended first into the lower parts of the earth?
He that decended is the same also that ascended up

far above all heavens, that he might fill all
things.) And he gave some, apostles; and some,
prophets; and some, evangelists; and some, pastors
and teachers...

Ephesians 4:8-12

Jim Bakker advertises his PTL Satellite Network as
"offering a free and better alternative" to most
secular television programming. As Bakker proudly
states in a brochure he sends to cable systems touting
the PTL Network, "Our network will help you satisfy
those millions of viewers who are tired of television's
sex and violence and those weary old movies. Our
uplifting and inspirational programming will be a
refreshing change to countless subscribers."2 Bakker
claims to have "the best in original programming, the
best in music and variety, the best in children's
programming," and "the best in teaching programs."
Under the category of "Original Programming," Bakker
includes "Teaching Seminars" with ministers, doctors,
lawyers, psychologists, and musicians; "Camp Meeting
USA" which features "down-home preaching and music;
"Jim Bakker and Friends," which is an interview program
with a magazine format; "Heritage USA Update," which
chronicles developments at PTL; and, of course, the
"Jim Bakker Show."

PTL's offerings under "Music and Variety" include
"Gospel Singing Jubilee," "The Blackwood Brothers," and
"More than a Song," a show that counts-down the Top 10
gospel songs. "Children's programming" includes such
shows as "Mr. Mustache," "Pirate Adventures," "Joy
Junction," and "Circle Square." Some of the children's
programs are live productions, and some are cartoon
shows. Under "Teaching Programs" Bakker includes such
offerings as Lester Sumrall, Zola Levitt, Dr. David
Lewis, Ray Brubaker, Mike Murdock, and others teaching
on topics as varied as Bible prophecy, angels and
demons, the Holy Land, financial security using God's
plan, and other subjects.

When one tunes in PTL, one gets more than basic
preaching by bright stars and rising stars. One also
gets Christian variety. It would take more space than
we have to discuss all of these shows, so we will
outline only a few in order to give the reader the

flavor of what is available in the category of Christian Variety programming.

Lester Sumrall: Teaching

Lester Sumrall is difficult to describe. He is not a handsome man, yet there is a certain quality of sincerity about him. Dr. Sumrall is a large person with a pronounced receding hairline. It is difficult, at least on television, to determine if his age has resulted in very much greying of his hair, because he clearly eschews the modern "dry look."

When the viewer tunes-in Dr. Sumrall for the first time, it is likely he or she will find it difficult to really take him seriously. The impulse is to snicker and turn off the television or change the channel. We suspect that the primary reason for such an attitude is the "unusual" subject matter of Dr. Sumrall's "lessons." The lessons are not typical, even for T.V. evangelicals. As far as we are aware, only Gary Greenwald's program entitled "The Eagle's Nest" deals with such esoteric topics. Dr. Sumrall has, in recent months, conducted "classes" on "demons and devils," including witches, warlocks, palm readers, charms, voodoo practitioners, evil spirits, and other manifestations of Satan in the world. In this series of lectures, he cautioned his students against wearing charm braclets, playing Dungeons and Dragons, or reading one's horoscope. To do these things is, according to Lester, to risk the devil inhabiting one's spirit and taking over one's life. In addition to the classes on "demons and devils," Lester recently completed 15 lessions on "Angels." During his classes on "angels," Dr. Sumrall discussed the history of angels in the biblical record, the types and forms of angels, their function(s) in modern society, and their current roles and functions in these, the "last days."

For the viewer who is not "born again" and "spirit filled," we imagine that it would be difficult to take seriously Dr. Sumrall's admonition that horoscopes are "the work of the devil." Yet, if the viewer watches Dr. Sumrall long enough, he becomes convinced of his unabiding devotion to the belief system he teaches. It is also clear that Dr. Sumrall enjoys teaching his unusual subjects, often smiling and chuckling at various points in his lessons and asking, "aren't we lucky to have Jesus." In one of his most recent series of lessons, Dr. Sumrall told of how he was dying of tuberculosis at the age of 17. Apparently, the Holy Spirit healed him, and because of this he has been led to share his knowledge of healing through a series of recent lessons entitled "Human Illness and Divine Healing: A Biblical Analysis of Sickness and Health." Dr. Sumrall never really solicits money; he ends his programs by simply outlining the various ways in which transcripts and/or tapes of a lecture can be obtained. He ends every program with a large, inviting smile and asks, "May I bless you?" He then prays for everyone in his class and for those who are watching the lesson on television. Dr. Sumrall really does want to "bless" his audience. Of all the T.V. preachers we have studied, Dr. Sumrall impresses us as the most elementary, and the most sincere.

Zola Levitt: Teaching

Zola Levitt is a Christian Jew. He appears to be in his late 40's or early 50's, has a very full beard and is beginning to become bald on the back of his head. He has a certain presence in front of the television camera. Zola is unlike any other T.V. preacher we have seen on Christian television. His show is entitled "Zola Levitt Live" and concentrates on low-keyed teaching, usually centered on Jesus, the Holy Land, Jewish history, and bible prophecy.

As often as not, the viewer will be treated to a tour of various locations in the Holy Land. When this happens, one will also shown pictures of such sites as the Wailing Wall, the Garden of Gethsame, the Island of Rhodes, Jesus' tomb, and other biblical locations. Zola is usually on location, adorned in the apparel of the people of Jesus' time. On one show we saw, Zola visited a wax museum with replicas of Jesus and his disciples at the Last Supper. As we watched, we hoped the heat of the camera lights would not harm the wax figures. There, among the wax models, was Zola, all decked-out in clothing like Jesus and his disciples.

Zola Levitt does teach; and while his penchant for

134

appearing in the dress of the time about which he is teaching seems to detract from his message, what Zola communicates is characterized by reason, rationality, and good sense. One doesn't laugh at Zola, in spite of appearing in gown, or robes, or sandals. We are impressed with the fact that Zola continually reminds his Christian television viewers that Jesus was a Jew. On one program Zola discussed the various ways in which different cultures represent Jesus' physical characteristics. He showed pictures of a Black Jesus, an Oriental Jesus, a Hispanic Jesus, a white, Anglo-Saxon, Protestant Jesus, and others. He then reminded his viewers that Jesus was, after all, a Jew, born and raised in the Middle-East, and that he must have looked much like Jewish natives of that area of the world. Zola then showed such a rendention of Jesus. We wondered, at the time, how those evangelical, born again Christians in his audience felt about the Zola's pictorial representation of Jesus.

Like all of the T.V. preachers, Zola needs money to stay on the air. Unlike most of the others, however, he doesn't harp on it, or make impassioned, "please save us from disaster" pleas. He does, like other T.V. preachers, offer premium inducements to encourage people to contribute money to his Dallas based ministry. While Zola claims that the quality of his premiums is better than run-of-the-mill "gifts," we are not so sure that such is the case. We are sure, however, that they are, in keeping with Zola himself, often unique when compared with what other Mass Media Ministers have to offer.

One thing that comes through on "Zola Levitt Live" is Zola's Jewish heritage. Zola closes every program by asking his viewers to "pray for the peace of Jerusalem."

John Ankerberg: Discussion

The John Ankerberg Show is the Christian television version of the Phil Donahue Show on secular T.V. In fact, John Ankerberg even looks something like Donahue; about the same physical frame and a head of blond hair. As far as we can tell, Ankerberg's show is designed to challenge all non-fundamentalist views of Christianity. The format is such that representatives of some

135

questionable group [by Ankerberg's reckoning] are
placed on a stage opposite some Christian expert(s).
The show generally proceeds with Ankerberg standing
among the audience, asking questions of the
non-Christian guests, and questions of the Christian
representatives. Topics such as "the new age movement,"
Mormonism, Jehovah's Witnesses, Cults, and other
movements are discussed, and typically shown to be
"false" or "dangerous." The telecasts are usually
interrupted at least once to make appeals for money or
to offer transcripts of the programs, books, or audio
tapes.

God's News Behind the News: Bible Prophecy

   Ray Brubaker's "God's News Behind the News" is
designed to resemble a secular newscast. The program
opens with scenes of troop movements, and armed
conflict; it then switches to Brubaker sitting at an
"anchor desk," where he begins to "report" on the news.
Brubaker frequently shifts to "special reports" on
special, critical areas of the world. The reports are
usually given by other members of the Brubaker family.
"God's News Behind the News" is a kind of quasi-bible
prophecy program in which the various wars, photos of
war ravaged people, and unsettled conditions in general
are used to predict the arrival of the Biblical "last
days." Brubaker's message is simple-- "please friend,
accept Jesus Christ as your Lord and Savior before it
is to late." Of course, such a message is wholly
consistent with Christian fundamentalism. "God's News
Behind the News" usually ends with Mrs. Brubaker
thanking the viewers for watching and asking for their
support.

The Way of the Winner: Teaching and Talk

   Mike Murdock is the "star" of "The Way of the
Winner," a Norman Vincent Peale, Power of Positive
Thinking kind of show. Murdock is a pianist, a song
composer, and a singer. He is an attractive man with
wavy hair, a well trimmed beard, and an attractive
physical build. The set of "The Way of the Winner"
consists of a piano, and a couch/coffee table area from
which Murdock teaches his viewers how to be a winner.

One of his favorite messages is on giving to the work of God and receiving God's rewards. Murdock says, over, and over, and over again, "You can't start receiving until you start giving." Murdock frequently talks about the viewer's "level of giving," (a term which refers to the $10, $100, $1000, etc. "level"). The message he teaches is that in order to increase the blessings one is receiving, one must first increase one's "level of giving." Mike reports on his giving $1,000 and receiving over $10,000 in return. According to Murdock, he has "received" [from God] such things as "priceless classic cars" and vans, not to mention large sums of money, because he has given of himself and his money, to God's work. Of course, Murdock asks for money, offering copies of his own record albums of Christian music as a premium inducement for a financial gift to his ministry. Murdock openly discusses his own divorce and the pain caused by the destruction of his family. According to Mike, he lost everything until he found the "way of the winner." What is that way? The Word of God. Know the word, use it principles, and you too will be a winner. Of course, in order to receive, you must give. Murdock makes sure that the viewer understands that giving to his ministry will set in motion the other side of the "giving equals receiving" equation.

More Than a Song: Music

Bob VanderMaten is the "star" of "More Than a Song." The show is designed to count-down the Top Ten gospel songs for the week. More Than a Song opens with VanderMaten appearing on stage in a tuxedo, announcing the format of the show and the weeks special musical guests who will perform live during the course of the telecast. VanderMaten is a tall, slender young man with brown hair, a broad smile, and sparkling eyes. His countenance is clearly happy, upbeat, and "born again."

The show proceeds with VanderMaten announcing the position of the Top Ten gospel songs for the current week as compared with the past week. When a song is announced, a video of the album cover or of the musical artist(s) performing a part of the song is flashed across the television screen. On occasion, VanderMaten or one of the PTL Singers will perform one of the ranked gospel songs. In between the position announcements for the various songs, the live musical guests perform. On the shows that we have seen, VanderMaten interviews all of the members of the guest musical group. He generally asks each person how he or she came to be a part of the group and how long they have been performing with the group. Many of those whom VanderMaten interviews give their personal testimonials. The live musical guests often comment on the many rewards of "singing and performing for Christ."

"More Than a Song" usually ends with VanderMaten and a guest announcing the number one gospel song for the week, followed by Bob singing a song of praise to the Lord. In our opinion the show is well staged, well performed, and entertaining. "More Than a Song" is telecast on the PTL Satellite Network at 11:00 PM (Eastern) on Sunday night.

Heritage USA Update: News

Heritage USA Update is a 30 minute program designed to showcase the building and expansion of Jim Bakker's Heritage USA Complex located just South of Charlotte, N.C. With this as its basic theme, the show always has more than ample material to present the viewer. This is because some construction or expansion always seems to be going on at Heritage USA.

The show opens with brief shots of the Heritage USA facility, Washington, D.C., and various sorts of construction machinery moving the earth, repairing pot-holes in roads, and/or putting up buildings. The montage is designed to create an image of a busy, growing, vibrant place. Every presentation of the building, expansion, and growth of Heritage USA is accompanied by fast-paced, upbeat music in the background. As far as we can tell, the show presents an accurate picture of activities at the Bakker complex.

When one watches the show, one is taken on a whirlwind tour of the PTL facility. There is a lot to see, and a lot to do at Heritage USA. In fact, in 1982, when Heritage USA was only three years old and much less extensive than it is today, The Saturday Evening Post described it as the "biggest bargain family vacation in Dixieland."3 According to The Saturday

138

Heritage USA is the kind of place you can go
for a week's vacation and never leave the
grounds. Once unpacked at a campsite or room,
fresh-faced teen-agers cheerfully escort you
around the place in open-air trams or
double-decker buses, all free of charge.

It's a place with an attitude all its own.
People talk nicer... cleaner. There are no
bars or beer cans. And cigarette smoke is
almost an Unidentified Flying Object in this
isolated center.

For kids of all ages, a village of log cabins
called "Recreation Village" offers an
impressive package of everything from
ping-pong and Pac-Man to basketball,
swimming, tennis, and horseshoes.

This may seem well and good for the kids and
hubbies, but what about moms? Obviously, no
one was left out, for the center offers an
amazing variety of shops.

Sounds impressive! Since the Saturday Evening Post
article was published, other construction has been
completed. The Upper Room, a replica of the Upper Room
in Jerusalem, a new Broadcast Center, and a new
"welcome center." Currently under construction are such
buildings as a "People That Love Home," which is a
facility designed to house pregnant girls and women who
do not want to have an abortion, a "Children's
Railroad," which will encircle Lake Heritage, and a $30
million complex called the "Heritage Grand" hotel. In
addition to the "Heritage Grand" with its 504 hotel
rooms, this new facility will also house some 60 shops
in a glass-encased area called "Mainstreet USA," a
cafeteria, and a large meeting hall. In all, the whole
facility will represent 11 acres under roof. It seems
as though Heritage USA Update really has something to
crow about!

The "Update" show also reports on the various other
facets of the PTL ministries, including the "People
That Love Centers," which are homes across the United
States designed to distribute clothes, food, shelter,
and temporary funds to people in need; PTL foreign

television broadcasts into at least 40 nations around the world; PTL world missions; the PTL Prison ministry, and other activities of the PTL programs. During the summer months large tour groups come to Heritage USA, and the Heritage USA Update show regularly interviews some of the folks who are a part of the tours. If one wishes to receive a factual, up-to-the-minute glimpse of what is going on at the Bakker facility, Heritage USA Update is the show to watch.

Lifeguide: Teaching

We have watched a lot of Christian television, and of all the programs we have tuned-in, Lifeguide is the most reasonable, rational, clear, concise, and believeable. Lifeguide features two men-- Phil Evanson of Tulsa, Oklahoma, and Gary Beauchamp of Dallas, Texas. Both are pastors of local Church of Christ congregations.

The program opens with pastors Evanson and Beauchamp sitting in chairs, situated on a carpeted area. That is all there is to the television set-- no flowers, no Christian art, no pianos, no singers, and no pulpit. All the viewers sees is two men sitting in chairs. Both Evanson and Beauchamp are well groomed, well dressed, pleasant looking persons. They present the appearance of thoughtful, intelligent, and concerned Christians. In a word, they are "believeable."

The program is usually centered on a single theme. A program may deal with marriage and the family, relating to children, caring for others, or a similar topic. Evanson and Beauchamp toss questions back and forth to each other on the topic at hand, discussing each others points in detail, and offering their own. They often acknowledge that their view of the world is sometimes "at odds" with that of other Christians, and non-Christians as well. Of course, their answers always lead the viewer back to the Bible and Jesus Christ. With Evanson and Beauchamp, however, it is a religious-intellectual voyage. While it is intellectual (and by this we mean that Evanson and Beauchamp do not insult the intelligence of the viewer by making rank appeals to human emotions), it is fundamental, basic Christianity.

140

As far as we can ascertain, Lifeguide originally featured only Phil Evanson; Beauchamp joined the program in 1983. He was, in our opinion, a solid addition.

Lifeguide offers a Bible study course, books, tapes, and a New International Verson of the New Testament, at no cost to the viewer. It is important to note that Evanson and Beauchamp never, and we mean never, ask for money. It seems to us that Lifeguide is probably the most clearly mainstream program on the PTL Satellite Network. It is, in our opinion, a program that has not compromised its religious integrity.

We suspect that when most Americans think of Christian television they conjure up images of Billy Graham, Oral Roberts, Pat Robertson, or one of the other well known T.V. preachers. We know that the majority of Americans do not watch Christian television and, therefore, most are probably unaware of the variety of offerings available on religious television. In this chapter we have provided the reader with a brief look at the variety of programs available to the viewer of religious television. Religious broadcasters are aware that all viewers are not attracted to evangelical preaching; they are also aware that they may be enticed to watch other programs that appear to be more intellectual, more entertaining, and more like secular T.V. than basic, straightforward preaching. They are aware, in other words, that they must try a variety of different forms of programming in order to get the "born again" message across. Trying they are, and from what we have observed,they are enjoying a good measure of success.

DOING GREAT EXPLOITS: WAKING THE MIGHTY MEN OF GOD

INTRODUCTION

Proclaim ye this among the Gentiles;
Prepare war, wake up the mighty men,
let all the men of war draw near; let
them come up.

Joel 3:9

Almost everyone who watches either religious or
secular television is aware that President Ronald
Reagan and the evangelicals of America have formed a
political mutual admiration society. Most citizens
probably believe that the wooing of the evangelicals by
Reagan began in the 1980 presidential campaign, tracing
the birth of that process back to Reagan's attendance
at the National Affairs Briefing in Dallas on August
22. The National Affairs Briefing was a New Christian

145

Right promotion managed by the [Religious] Roundtable. While Reagan's comments on the theory of evolution at a press conference following the meeting were to play an important part in assuring the backing of the evangelicals, they were not, in themselves, the beginning of the Reagan/evangelical relationship.

REAGAN AND THE EVANGELICALS: ESTABLISHING A RELATIONSHIP

Blow ye the trumpet in Zion and
sound an alarm in my holy mountain;
let all the inhabitants of the land
tremble for the day of the Lord
cometh, for it is nigh at hand.

Joel 2:1

Richard V. Pierard suggests that a "systematic effort on the part of evangelical conservatives to portray Reagan as a man of faith began during his governorship [of California]."1 If this is the case, the affectivity of Reagan for the evangelicals, and vice-versa, began some 14 to 15 years before the 1980 presidential campaign. Apparently, Reagan announced his intentions to bring basic religious precepts to bear on secular, governmental affairs in his inaugural address as Governor of California. Reagan "quoted Benjamin Franklin as saying that any man who dared to bring the teachings of Jesus Christ into public office would revolutionize the world, and declared that he would `try very hard'" to do just that.2 In a statement that seems to have added to the cordiality of his relationship with the evangelicals, Reagan told a reporter that he had received Christ and given his life to Him prior to his election to the California governorship. He also said that "I've always believed there is a certain divine scheme of things. I'm not quite able to explain how my election happened or why I'm here, apart from believing it is part of God's plan for me."3 It seems, therefore, that the mutual courting between Reagan and the evangelicals had an earlier beginning than most people are aware or believe.

146

In 1975, Bill Bright, of the Campus Crusade for Christ joined with John B. Conlan, Republican Congressman from Arizona, and other notable evangelicals to orchestrate an effort to elect conservative Christians to public office during the 1976 elections. As it turned out, the effort involved the coordinated efforts of three groups-- the Christian Freedom Foundation, Third Century Publishers, and Bill Bright's "Christian Embassy" in Washington, D.C. According to Pierard, "these forces were to constitute the evangelical vanguard of a Reagan presidential bid."4 Following these efforts were a number of additional maneuvers designed to enhance the image of Ronald Reagan as a man of faith, and to make him publically and politically acceptable to mainstream, evangelical Christianity. Among these other efforts was a campaign tract prepared by Charles Hobbs; a tract interestingly entitled "Ronald Reagan's Call to Action." Pierard reports that George Otis, the host of a charasmatic talk-show, interviewed Ronald Reagan about his position on "spiritual and moral issues," on Otis' television program.5 Apparently the program was "widely publicized in the evangelical press and conveyed the distinct impression that Reagan was one of them."6 So it seems that the evangelicals began to come together for Ronald Reagan (or to "come against" liberal democrats) in the Reagan bid for the 1976 presidential nomination of the Republican party. The evangelicals did not, however, succeed in their efforts on Reagan's behalf. Although they did not prevail with Reagan in 1976, they had clearly established Ronald Reagan as a solid candidate of the evangelical community. Perhaps it was through the "trials of fire" in the 1976 campaign that the real muscle of what is now called the "New Christian Right," was forged and formed.

The New Christian Right flexed its muscle in the 1978 senatorial elections, drawing the attention and approval of several conservative secular groups. As a result of these initial successes, the New Christian Right coalesced from three identifiable groups-- Christian Voice, Moral Majority, and the [Religious] Roundtable. As Hadden and Swann, Pierard, and others have commented, the formation of these groups made "born again" politics an important political reality in America.7

REAGAN AND THE EVANGELICALS: THE '80 CAMPAIGN

And the Lord shall utter his voice
before his army: for his camp is very
great: for he is strong that executeth
his word: for the day of the Lord is
great and very terrible and who can
abide it?

Joel 2:11

Of course, Reagan was not getting any younger, a
problem of some concern to the evangelicals. His age
was a problem in the sense that they hoped that he
would make a run for the Republican nomination again in
1980. To that end, John Conlan began sponsoring
fund-raisers to enlist the personal and financial
backing of Christian businessmen and professional
people for a second Reagan run for the nomination. In
March of 1980, at the convention of the National
Association of Evangelicals, Congressman Conlan
personally distributed a leaflet titled "Ronald Reagan:
A Man of Faith," to the evangelicals in attendance at
the convention. In addition, Adrian Rogers, pastor of a
large Southern Baptist church in Memphis, talked with
Ronald Reagan during the primary campaign and opined
that he found Reagan to be a man of God, to have
accepted Christ, and to be an acceptable candidate. It
seems that early in the primary campaign the New
Christian Right was getting behind candidate Reagan.
The years of interaction that began back in the days
before the run for the California governorship seemed
to be bearing political fruit for both Reagan and the
evangelicals.

Jimmy Carter is an avowed born-again Christian, and
he had done well with the evangelical community in the
1976 election. Because of this, Reagan apparently felt
that it was time to openly and publically line-up his
candidacy with the evangelicals. Pollster Richard
Wirthlin's announcement that Reagan had an edge among
Protestants who had made a personal commitment to
Christ, and that these voters would keep Jimmy Carter
from "cornering the born-again market" in the South and

in such swing states as Ohio and Illinois, was probably an important political catalyst in the decision to intensify the courting of the born-again vote. Thus, on May 26, 1980, Reagan was asked at a press conference whether he was a born-again Christian. Reagan's reply was:8

> Well, I know what many of those who use that term mean by it. But in my own situation it was not in the religion, or the church that I was raised in, the Christian Church. But there you were baptized when you yourself decided that you were as the Bible says, as the Bible puts it, that that is being born again. Within the context of the Bible, yes, by being baptized.

Following the press conference, candidate Reagan consented to being interviewed by Jim Bakker on the PTL Sattelite Network. The interview also appeared in Bakker's magazine entitled, at that time, Action. After the May 26 press conference, over 200 Protestant ministers came together on June 24 in Atlanta. Two things came out of the Atlanta meeting. First, the ministers formed the Georgia Pastors Forum. Second, the pastors heard Paul Weyrich (Weyrich was a major player in the formation of the Moral Majority, in 1979) and others criticize Jimmy Carter as a "humanist"; they were then given instructions on how to organize themselves and their churches to defeat Carter and elect Ronald Reagan.

On the heels of the June meeting in Atlanta came the Republican National Convention in Detroit, in July. At the convention, the evangelicals, primarily through Jerry Falwell representing the Moral Majority, exercised significant influence on some of the planks in the Reagan platform. As a result of the evangelical input, the platform contained an anti-abortion plank and an anti-ERA plank. Falwell also opposed George Bush as Reagan's running mate, an opposition that was not heeded. But candidate Reagan would still have something to give the evangelicals, and it further cemented their support for him. There were enough evangelicals at the convention that Reagan knew he could not ignore them. Before the national convention, for example, the Alaska Moral Majority had captured the Republican convention in that state; as a result, the Alaska delegation (like some others) was composed of mostly evangelicals.

149

During his speech accepting the nomination as the Republican standard-bearer for the nation's highest office, Reagan said:9

> Can we doubt that only a Divine Providence placed this land, this island of freedom, here as a refuge for all those people in the world who yearn to breathe free? . . . I'll confess that I've been a little afraid to suggest what I'm going to suggest. I'm more afraid not to. Can we begin our crusade joined together in a moment of silent prayer? [Pause] God bless America.

In these few comments in his acceptance speech, Reagan succesfully baited the evangelical hook.

With the Republican nomination wrapped-up, Reagan hit the campaign trail. However, he apparently felt the need to further solidify his support among the evangelical community. Thus, on August 22, candidate Reagan attended the [Religious] Roundtable sponsored National Affairs Briefing in Dallas, Texas. At the beginning of this chapter we suggested that "Reagan's comments on the theory of evolution [at the Roundtable press conference] . . . .were to play an important part in assuring the backing of the evangelicals." What he said at that press conference was not particularly profound or unequivocal, but the evangelicals loved it:10

> I have a great many questions about it. I think that recent discoveries have pointed up great flaws. . . . It is a theory, it is a scientific theory only, and it has in recent years been challenged in the world of science and it is not yet believed in the scientific community to be as infallible as it once was believed.

Speaking to the more than 15,000 faithful at the National Affairs Briefing, Reagan told the evangelicals, "I know you can't endorse me. But . . . I want you to know that I endorse you." However, not all of the evangelicals shared Reagan's appeal for a marriage between evangelicals and political action. Pat Robertson, president of CBN, has suggested that "active partisan politics" is not the correct approach for true evangelicals. According to Robertson "There's a better way. Fasting and praying. . . appealing, in essence, to a higher power."11 Robertson's voice was, however, only one of a very few unenthusiastic voices to be heard.

If Reagan's acceptance speech baited the evangelical hook, his comments on the theory of evolution yanked the line, and Reagan reeled the evangelicals aboard the Reagan political ship. The rest is history, Reagan catapulted to a surprisingly easy victory over Jimmy Carter in the November, 1980, general election.

REAGAN AND THE EVANGELICALS: THE `84 CAMPAIGN

And the children of Isachar which were
men that had understanding of the times,
to know what Israel ought to do, the heads
of them were two hundred, and all their
brethren were at their commandment.

I Chron. 12:32

President Reagan opened his 1984 bid for reelection to the nation's highest political office by "aligning himself more closely than ever before with conservative Christian moral causes."12 In order to accomplish this closer alignment, Reagan addressed the convention of the National Religious Broadcasters (NRB), a group of some 4,000 conservative Christians. What is the NRB? It is made up of more than 1,000 organizations devoted to producing religious radio and television programs, operating religious radio, television, and cable stations, and broadcasting the conservative Christian message via satellite. Religious broadcasting is a rapidly growing industry. In commenting on it's rapid growth, Christianity Today said the following:13

> Last year the number of television stations
> with a religious format increased 21
> percent, from 65 to 79. The number of
> religious radio stations increased 13
> percent, from 922 to 1,045. The number of

151

firms producing religious television programs and films for use in the United States increased 30 percent, from 280 to 365.

The NRB has an openly conservative, evangelical focus; a focus which it uses as it represents 75 percent of the religious broadcast industry in the United States. If Reagan wanted to get closer to the evangelicals in America, therefore, it is easy to see why he would choose to speak to the group that manages the religious media.

According to Christianity Today, "Reagan's 25-minute speech to the broadcasters was interrupted 23 times by applause, including six thunderous, standing ovations. The longest was in response to his quotation of John 3:16, with it unequivocating declaration of belief in Jesus Christ as Savior and provider of eternal life."14 In using that verse, especially given the context of the speech, Reagan seems to have told the religious broadcasters that he moved squarely into the camp of evangelical Christianity. In a way, his statement could be taken as a sort of public witnessing. A few brief quotes from his speech to the NRB will suffice to illustrate the idea of a public witnessing.15

> "Nineteen eighty-three was the year more of us read the Good Book. Can we make a resolution here today: That 1984 will be the year we put its great truths into action?

> "My experience in this office I hold has only deepend a belief I've held for many years: Within the covers of that single Book are all the answers to all the problems that face us today-- if only we'd read and believe...

> "I know what I am about to say now is controversial, but I have to say it. This nation cannot continue turning a blind eye and a deaf ear to the taking of some 4,000 unborn children's lives every day. That's one every 21 seconds. We cannot pretend America is preserving her first and highest ideal-- the belief that each life is sacred-- when we have permitted the death of 15 million helpless innocents since the

Roe v. Wade decision.

"Fifteen million children who will never laugh, never sing, never know the joy of human love; will never strive to heal the sick, feed the poor, or make peace among nations. Abortion has denied them the most basic of human rights. We are all infinitely poorer for their loss....

"Restoring the right to life and protecting people from violence and exploitation are important responsibilities. But as members of God's family we share another-- helping to build a foundation of faith and knowledge to prepare our children for the challenges of life. `Train up a child in the way he should go,' Solomon wrote, `and when he is old he will not depart from it.'

"Teddy Roosevelt told us, `The American people are slow to wrath, but when their wrath is once kindled, it burns like a consuming flame,' I think Americans are getting angry. I think they have a message, and Congress better listen: We are a government of, by, and for the people. And people want a constitutional amendment making it unequivocally clear our children can hold voluntary prayer in every school across this land. And if we could get God and discipline back in our schools, may be we could get drugs and violence out. I know that some believe prayer in schools should be restricted to a moment of silence. Well, we already have the right to remain silent. We need a new amendment to restore the rights that were taken from us. Senator [Howard] Baker has assured us we will get a vote on our amendment. And that will be a great victory for our children.

"`For God so loved the world, that he gave his only begotten Son, that whosoever believeth in him should not perish, but have everlasting life.' I'm a little self-conscious, because I know you all could recite that verse to me. Helping each other, believing in Him, we need never be afraid. We will be part of something far more powerful, enduring, and good than all the forces here on earth. We will be part of paradise. May God keep you always, and may you always keep God."

The theme of the NRB convention was "Facing the Issues." As Christianity Today suggests, "no speaker faced them more directly than Reagan."16

In its April 6, 1984 issue, Christianity Today published an article entitled "Once Again, Reagan Pitches for Evangelical Support."17 The article began with the following words:18

During the past year, the National Association of Evangelicals (NAE) has received national attention unrivaled in its 42-year history. And there is one person to thank for the increased public notice: President Ronald Reagan.

In 1984 Reagan returned to the NEA's convention in Columbus, Ohio. He was welcomed with open arms by the 1,800 evangelicals in attendance.

Christianity Today went on to report:

The President told the evangelical Christians that "America has begun a spiritual awakening." And he challenged the audience to be tolerant of differing viewpoints. "Please use your pulpits to denounce racism, anti-Semitism, and all ethnic or religious intolerance as evils. . .

He repeated his opposition to abortion, Challenging Christians to find "positive solutions" to the problem. He reiterated his support for group prayer in public schools, tuition tax credits, and a strong national defense.

One of three standing ovations followed Reagan's call for evangelical support of the

proposed school prayer amendment. He also
asked the audience to support a bill that
would give students the right to use public
school facilities for religious purposes. The
following day, convention delegates passed a
resolution supporting both measures.

Perhaps Democrats, liberals, and non-evangelicals
would disagree with the way in which President Reagan
"faced the issues" at the NRB and the NAE conventions;
Reagan, however, has clearly seen the light and
assessed the power of religious broadcasting, and he is
counting on the Electronic Church to preach, teach,
talk, and telecast on his behalf. His public position
on religious matters has been made crystal clear. An
important question is whether the public will'vote for
that position to be again manifest in the White House
for the next four years.

JERRY FALWELL: THE "MORAL MAJORITY"

And if ye go to war in your land against
the enemy that oppresseth you, then ye
shall blow an alarm with the trumpets; and
ye shall be saved from your enemies.

Numbers 10:9

The headline on the cover of the September 15, 1980,
issue of Newsweek spelled-out "Born-Again Politics."
The cover featured, in large block letters, the word
"vote," with the letter "T" in the word enlarged to
resemble the Christian Cross. And there, in the middle
of the enlarged "T," was a photograph of the Rev. Jerry
Falwell. The featured article was entitled "A Tide of
Born-Again Politics"; it began with the following
words.19

The Rev. Jerry Falwell fidgeted impatiently
as he waited for a colleague to finish

155

thanking the Lord for his bounty. Finally,
the Wednesday evening prayer service almost
at an end, Falwell strode to the pulpit to
address the well-scrubbed congregation of
3,900 that filled the Thomas Road Baptist
Church in Lynchburg, Va., a fortnight ago.
"Senator [Mike] Gravel of [Alaska] was
ousted last night," he told them. "He lost
the primary. And that's the beginning."
Before the year was out, Falwell intoned, a
half dozen more liberal senators would fall:
George McGovern of South Dakota and Frank
Church of Idaho, John Culver of Iowa and
Alan Cranston of California, Birch Bayh of
Indiana and Gaylord Nelson of Wisconsin.
"The moralists in America have had enough.
[We] are joining hands together for the
changing, the rejuvenating of a nation."

Falwell was not completely accurate in his predictive
statements regarding the outcome of those senatorial
races; but he was close enough to generate significant
media attention when the election dust had settled.
When the ballots had all been counted, Falwell had
missed the mark only once-- Alan Cranston of California
had survived. Much of the liberal leadership of the
senate had, however, been defeated. Along with the
defeats of McGovern, Church, Culver, Bayh, and Nelson,
came the election of more conservative replacements
and, of course, Ronald Reagan as President of the
United States. Ronald Reagan's victory was not a great
surprise-- the inundating of the liberal leadership of
the senate was, however, a truly unexpected outcome of
the election.

After the election came the inevitable questions.....
Why?.....How? Jerry Falwell believed that he knew the
"whys" and "hows," and he wasted very little time in
telling Americans that the defeats and the victories
were wrought by the mighty hand of the Moral Majority.
The pollster Lou Harris and the secular press were, by
and large, quick to agree with Falwell. As the news of
the wishes of the electorate exploded on the public
imagination, the desire to know more about Falwell and
the Moral Majority grew quickly.

The Moral Majority was born on a summer day in June,
1979. The political activity of Jerry Falwell, however,
predated the birth of the Moral Majority by quite some

time. For example, in 1976, the year of America's bicentennial, students at Falwell's Liberty Baptist College performed at "I Love America" rallies in 112 major cities around the country. The year 1978 saw the Falwell ministry initiate the "Clean Up America" Campaign. According to Falwell, "The overwhelming conservative views of those responding to the survey were sent to decision-makers across the nation."20 In April, 1979, two months before the birth of Moral Majority, Falwell himself held the first "I Love America" rally at the Capital in Washington, D.C. "The program was filmed and produced as the first prime-time television special aired by the Old-Time Gospel Hour. In September the `I Love America' Rally began its two-year tour of the 50 state capitals..."21 According to the Falwell ministry:22

> National press continually focused attention on Jerry Falwell. Through his book Listen America!, and his rousing sermons at "I Love America" Rallies, Jerry Falwell reinforced the need for America to return to "moral sanity."

The "moral sanity" Falwell spoke about was reflected in his "agenda for the `80s" for the Moral Majority. In essence, the Moral Majority seemed to be against more than it was for. Of course, Falwell and the Moral Majority would probably respond that they must be against many evils in American society in order to protect the things that they are for-- the family, preservation of infant human life, and traditional morals. In order to make certain that what they support will have a fighting chance to survive, The Moral Majority actively opposes such things as abortion on demand, the ERA, homosexual rights, drug usage, pornography, and other issues. Falwell and the Moral Majority also support prayer in public schools and equal access to public school facilities for religious groups. As of this moment, however, these two issues supported by the Moral Majority have been voted down in the U.S. Congress. Even though the two issues lost in the Congress, President Reagan is not letting the T.V. preachers forget that he at least put the legislation forward. For example, on May 21, 1984, Jim Bakker announced that he had received a letter from the President thanking him for his help and support in the prayer in school bill. Of course, Bakker looked into the camera and said that we should be thankful for the President.

Moral Majority is a political organization, not a religious one. The men who came up with the idea for a Christian political movement were not preachers; they were, in fact, political professionals. According to Newsweek, the core members of the new political organization were Howard Phillips, organizer of the Conservative Caucus, Paul Weyrich, Robert Billings, (a GOP congressional candidate who lost in Indiana), and Ed McAteer.23 McAteer was "a veteran marketing man for the Colgate-Palmolive Co. who had come to know hundreds of evangelical preachers around the country."24 These men prevailed on Falwell to set up and represent the Moral Majority, and he agreed to do so.

After agreeing to be the banner-carrier of Moral Majority, Falwell began to hold rallies around the nation to enlist members. During the 1980 election, Falwell claimed that the Moral Majority had as many as 3 million voters on its roles. As it turns out, however, this number seems to be as overstated as are the claims of audience size for the Old-Time Gospel Hour. We do not, however, wish to rehash this issue once again. Suffice it to say that since the election in 1980 many Americans have been convinced that the Moral Majority is a politically potent force, and one that is rapidly becoming a politically powerful.

The Moral Majority seems to be gaining some political saavy in the use of disruptive techniques. Since its inception in 1979, Jerry Falwell has steadfastly claimed that the Moral Majority is not allied with any particular party. However, the actions of Moral Majority in May, 1984, make that position difficult to accept. During May, the Moral Majority sent out an "urgent" mailgram to its list of 100,000 supporters residing in states east of the Mississippi river, suggesting that they take certain actions that would prove to be disruptive to the Democratic telethon. What did the mailgram say?:

> Please help! Democratic National Committee (DNC) plans to use the telethon to raise between $8 and $10 million to elect liberal, anti-family, pro-homosexual, pro-nuclear freeze, pro-abortion candidates.

The Moral Majority suggested that supporters do three things: (1) be sure and watch the telethon, (2) call the telethon number and "let them know that you support the President and resent their slanted distortions," and (3) "send a gift of $15 to Moral Majority." "Ann Lewis, political director for the DNC, fielded calls in California during the telethon. `I received four hand-ups or anti-Democratic calls for every pledge.'" Lewis' ratio was, according to computer records, consistent with what happened throughout the country.

While Moral Majority claims to be nonpartisan, its actions, and the words of its spokesmen seem to suggest otherwise. Moral Majority spokesman Cal Thomas (a former NBC correspondent in Washington, D.C.) said "In our judgement the Democratic party tragically has been taken over by ultra-left-wing interest groups." If Moral Majority is to be believed, those interest groups are anti-family, pro-homosexual, pro-nuclear freeze, and pro-abortion. We find these accusations interesting, especially in view of the fact that Gallup polls show that 57 percent of evangelicals view themselves as Democrats.

Recent evidence, however, does not substantiate such belief in the power, pervasiveness, and influence of the Moral Majority. Anson Shupe and William A. Stacy have completed research on the Moral Majority through two surveys conducted in the Dallas-Ft. Worth area.25 Shupe and Stacy surveyed the area's general population and its local ministers to assess the strength of grass roots support for the Moral Majority. Edward P. Freeland, in a review of the Shupe and Stacy research states that the research confirmed "what many have suspected all along: that the media attention given to leaders of the New Religious Right and their respective organizations is far out of proportion to their base of popular support."26 As Freeland reports, "those who oppose Falwell's organization outnumber its supporters by about a two to one margin."27 As one reads Freeland's review, one gets the impression that such data suggest very little support for Moral Majority. We, however, are impressed with the fact that one-third of the respondents do not oppose Falwell's organization!

Shupe and Stacy also examined the religious and political correlates of the Moral Majority movement and found that involvement in the electronic church was closely related to attitudes toward the Moral Majority. In other words, those with the most favorable attitudes were likely to watch Christian television, the very medium Falwell has used to create the image of Moral Majority as a large socio-political movement with a well organized following adhering to the basic beliefs of the organization. It is instructive to note that Shupe and Stacy make the point that only a small portion of the sample they studied watch the overtly political T.V. preachers. This suggests that the apparent success of the Moral Majority is a result of highly successful "impression management" through the use of mass media, and not a result of broad based public support. While Shupe and Stacy's study suggests that the Moral Majority is not as monolithic as Falwell or the media would have us belive, Freeland does raise some vexing questions in his review of their work:28

> Yet this book seems to raise as many questions as it resolves. Indeed perhaps its greatest flaw is its brevity: much of their data seems to beg for further speculation. For instance, there are a substantial number of conservatives in the sample who haven't yet made up their minds about the Moral Majority or haven't heard of it. One wonders what chain of events might lead them to support those organizations with which, for the most part, they are already in agreement. Much of the data seems to evince a great deal of latent support for the New Religious Right.

> Furthermore, public support is only one of the many factors that can make or break a social movement organization. No other social movement in our history has had as much access to the major communications media as does the New Religious Right.

What Freeland seems to be saying is that while the evidence points to less than a floodtide of popular support for Moral Majority, smugness and ridicule should not set-in for those who oppose the platform of the organization. With the right series of events, Moral Majority could cascade on the American political scene with the "twinkling of the T.V. eye."

PAT ROBERTSON: "THE FREEDOM COUNCIL"

Of Zebulum such went forth to battle,
expert in war, with all instruments of
war, fifty thousand, which could keep
rank: they were not of double heart.

I Chron. 12:35

The "Freedom Council" is a CBN sponsored organization
designed to make certain that "no longer will
legislators be able to say, `Nothing will happen if I
cross the Christians."29 On April 5, 1984, we received
a letter from Pat Robertson, on CBN letterhead. In that
letter Robertson said:30

> God gave us the concept of The Freedom
> Council in the first place. And since that
> time He has continued to open door after
> door to bring us all the resources we need
> to make The Freedom Council a powerful voice
> for religious liberty in this nation.

Given Robertson's own words, one might conclude that
The Freedom Council's major goal is to protect
religious liberty. However, enclosed with Robertson's
letter was volume two, number two, of a publication
entitled "The Freedom Report." The Freedom Report is,
apparently, a Newsletter published by The Freedom
Council and sent to all members of the organization. In
that publication, Ted Pantaleo, executive director of
The Freedom Council, stated:31

> As soon as we complete the Precinct Plan we
> can field a vast nationwide army for the
> Lord that can pray, lobby, evangelize,
> conduct voter registration drives or do
> anything in concert that may be needed.

Pantaleo's words seem to suggest that The Freedom
Council wants to register voters to make certain that
something will happen to a politician if he or she

doesn't vote the right way,or chooses to "cross the Christians." In fact, "The Freedom Report" document we received devoted a significant amount of space to detailing "Phase II" of The Freedom Council plan. "Phase II" is "The Precinct Plan," a plan to organize 175,561 Precinct Coordinators in local home districts. According to The Freedom Council Report, "when voting, [legislators] are swayed by what they feel is the over whelming sentiments in their home districts-- the overwhelming sentiments of those who will act on them, that is."32 Apparently, The Freedom Council intends to try to make sure that conservative Christians are among those who will act on their sentiments. Accomplishing such a task will not be as difficult as it sounds:33

> Finding the more than 180,000 Christian leaders needed around the nation could seem like an impossibly large task. But the Precinct Plan breaks it down into realistic portions. Under the Precinct Plan no one person is responsible for finding any more than seven people who will join The Freedom Council in working to preserve religious freedom. In this way a powerful grassroots organization will be formed.

It is difficult to assess the political aspirations of Robertson for The Freedom Council. Robertson has, in the past, expressed some general uneasiness about the evangelicals playing an active role in political affairs. "`God isn't a right-winger or a left-winger,' argues preacher Pat Robertson, president of the Christian Broadcasting Network and host of `The 700 Club,' a popular daily religious program. `The evangelists stand in danger of being used and manipulated.'"34 That doesn't sound like an evangelical political activist to us. Yet, Pat has expressed the activist theme on The 700 Club: "We have enough votes to run the country. . . .And when the people say `we've had enough,' we are going to take over the country."35 Perhaps Pat feels that the people are beginning to say "we've had enough," and the creation of The Freedom Council is his way of responding to their cries. As suggested earlier in this book, Robertson's 700 Club theme for this year is "America at the Crossroads." Perhaps The Freedom Council plans to be a force in deciding whether the country will take the "same old road," or the "road less traveled."

DOING GREAT EXPLOITS: CHURCH VS STATE

And I beheld when he had opened the
sixth seal, and, lo, there was a
great earthquake; and the sun became
black as sackcloth of hair, and the
moon became as blood. And the stars
of heaven fell unto the earth, even
as a fig tree casteth her untinely
figs, when she is shaken of a mighty
wind. And the heaven departed as a
scroll when it is rolled together;
and every mountain and island were
moved out of their places. And the
kings of the earth, and the great
men, and the rich men, and the chief
captains, and the mighty men, and
every bond man, and every free man,
hid themselves in the dens and in
the rock of the mountains; And said
to the mountains and rocks, Fall on
us, and hide us from the face of him
that sitteth on the throne, and from
the wrath of the Lamb: For the great
day of his wrath is come; and who
shall be able to stand?

Revelation 6:12-17

In its March 5, 1984 issue, U.S. News and World
Report indicated that there are 1,200 court cases
involving church and state currently being watched by
The Christian Legal Society. According to John Baker,
general counsel of the Baptist Joint Committee on
Public Affairs, "I have never seen so many church-state
battles. They have opened some of the old wounds
between Protestant and Catholic and North and South.
Tempers are very short."36 The 1,200 cases represent a
6 fold increase in contests between church and state
than were taking place just one decade ago. As we
ponder this dramatic increase in church-state battles,

163

we are reminded of the Biblical admonition in Mark
12:17, to "render to Caesar the things that are
Caesar's, and to God the things that are God's."
Clearly, there is a difference of opinion regarding
what is Cesar's and what is God's in America. The
television preachers say that the war over what should
be rendered to whom is a war with the servants of the
devil.

What does this increasing battle portend for
American society? It quite obviously means a battle to
be waged with the courts, with computers, satellites,
television, and with ballot boxes. For those who would
discount the importance of the current struggle in our
society, we remind them of the Protestant Reformation
and its effect on the societies of Europe. We are not
saying that televangelism will have such an effect on
American society, but we are also aware that Martin
Luther did not have television, computers, or
satellites. In the case of the Protestant Reformation,
class and social conflict raged throughout much of
Europe, including England. Whole new religious groups
came out of this period of turmoil. The affairs of
nations were affected. The Roman Catholic Church,
seeing its influence diminishing, launched the
Counter-Reformation, resulting in (among other things)
the inquisition and subsequent persecution. Our
position is not that of an alarmist, although we, like
John Baker, are somewhat disturbed by the developing
situation. Our position is that the T.V. preachers want
changes in American society which are not desired the
majority of Americans, and which will have the backing
and force of the television preachers and their rather
large following.

The backdrop for the developing controversy between
church and state is the first amendment to the U.S.
constitution. The first amendment states, in part, that
"Congress shall make no law respecting an establishment
of religion, or prohibiting the free exercise
thereof..." The T.V. preachers claim that the first
amendment is directly related to the religious and
political issues in which they are interested.

A glance at any high school textbook in American
history reveals a long history of different
interpretations of, and reactions to, the first
amendment. The assumptions about the meaning of this
amendment have had the effect of banning organized

164

prayer in public schools. This, of course, offends the T.V. preachers, and they suggest that it offends the majority of the American public, as well. The T.V. preachers say that recent polls demonstrate that over 80 percent of the American public favors prayer in public schools. Yet, in a recent vote on a proposed amendment to the constitution to allow voluntary prayer in public schools, the Senate failed to get the number of votes needed to send the bill to the House of Representatives. President Reagan sent the proposed amendment to the Senate and made public statements supporting its passage. He even appeared on Jim Bakker's PTL Club Show, Pat Robertson's 700 Club Show, and Jerry Falwell's "Spiritual State of the Union Address," asking evangelicals to support the legislation. Forty-four U.S. Senators opposed the bill and in so doing, raised the anger of the T.V. preachers. We recently saw the Rev. Hilton Sutton, a Bible prophecy preacher, say on Bakker's PTL Satellite Network, "We are going to put those Senators who voted against the prayer amendment out of a job." He got a rousing ovation from the audience. We believe that Sutton's statement provides a good summary of the sentiment of the majority of the T.V. preachers.

There is another issue which brings the government and religion into confrontation. This is the question of religious schools of all denominations. Most people are aware that there have been Roman Catholic parochial schools for many decades in this country. Most people are also aware that the parents of students who attend these schools not only pay local school taxes to the government to support public schools, but they also pay tuition for their children's parochial education. Over the years, many Roman Catholic's have not been particularly pleased with this situation.

What many people may not be aware of is that enrollment in non-traditional church schools has risen from 209,000 in 1970, ·to about one million in 1984.37 According to U.S. News and World Report, there are about 20,000 fundamentalist schools in America, and the number increases by three schools each day.38 Given the fact that the U.S. Supreme Court upheld a Minnesota law which allows parents to get deductions on their state taxes for their children's school expenses, we believe that further storms are brewing on the horizon of relations between religious backed schools and those who perceive such tax credits as support for established religion and a violation of the first amendment. The lines of battle are being drawn between those people who fear the erosion of the concept of the total separation of church state, and those who believe that America is a God established society and that the "secular humanists" are exercising undue influence in reducing the freedom of religion.

The American Civil Liberties Union (ACLU) is one organization which fights the mixing of religion and the functional institutions of government. On a segment of the 700 Club, we saw Pat Robertson say that he was "going against" the ACLU because of their ungodliness. It is safe to say that other T.V. preachers are not happy about the actions of the ACLU. In a speech to the National Religious Broadcasters (NRB), the President said that he was in full support of their goals for religion in American life. President Reagan was criticized by the ACLU for declaring 1983 the "Year of the Bible." While addressing the NRB Reagan told the evangelical broadcasters that he wore the ACLU's criticism like "a badge of honor."

On the Good Friday evening broadcast of the 700 Club, Pat Robertson reported that Larry Flint's Hustler magazine had just published an issue showing a nude woman on a cross. According to Robertson, the Mayor of Philadelphia banned the magazine in the city. Pat went on to say that the ACLU had issued a statement claiming that this banning of Hustler magazine was a clear violation of the separation of church and state. We leave the legal arguments to the many lawyers in this country. However, from the standpoint of the sensitivity of religious people in America, many are incensed by the ACLU statement. Many people undoubtedly agree with the T.V. preachers who call for an end to the open publishing of this type of material.

Many Americans have heard it said that the U.S. Supreme Court is a continuing constitutional convention. As it has worked out in American society, this indeed seems to be the case. The process of passing a constitutional amendment by the Congress, and the signing of the bill by the President after the individual states have ratified the amendment, is long and uncertain. Proponents of the Equal Rights Amendment (ERA) can attest to this fact. Thus, if the prayer amendment had passed the Senate in the Spring of 1984, it could have been as late as 1991 before final action

166

could be taken to make the amendment the law of the land. However, a Supreme Court decision on an issue can be immediately binding on the entire country. It is safe to assume that the lawyers of religious organizations that want changes are aware of the power of the Supreme Court. We would not be surprised, therefore, to see test cases before the Supreme Court dealing with issues of church and state. We would be surprised if these cases did not bring to light the hostility that the fundamentalists and the so-called "secular-humanists" have for one another.

The issues we have been discussing are a part of the very fabric of American society. Harvey Cox, a noted theologian at Harvard University, apparently agrees that something is afoot regarding the fundamentalist movement in America. In an interview with U.S. News and World Report, Cox said, "Make no mistake about it, the fundamentalist movement is to be taken very seriously."39 Dr. Cox has long had his hand on the pulse of religion in America, and his admonition should be taken to heart.

As we have noted, the T.V. preachers are of one mind in their continuing efforts to promote prayer and Bible reading in public schools, to bring an end to abortion on demand, to end the proliferation of pornography, and to promote allowing Christian schools to operate with a minimum of government regulation and "interference."

A recent evangelical effort in California can be used to demonstrate the determination and power of evangelicals to get what they want.

In March of 1984, Governor George Deukmejian of California vetoed a bill designed to protect homosexuals from employment discrimination. Although the bill had passed both the state senate and assembly, the floor debate over the measure had been lively and spirited. Upon passage of the bill, a Sacramento-based organization called the "Committee on Moral Concerns" orchestrated a drive to cause Governor Deukmejian to veto the bill. According to Christianity Today, "Gov. George Deukmejian was swamped by nearly 100,000 phone calls and letters-- thought to be the most ever received by a California governor on a single subject."40

W.B. Timberlake, a former Southern Baptist preacher

and lawyer, headed the Committee on Moral Concerns, and spearheaded the veto effort. Art Croney, associate lobbyist for the Committee on Moral Concerns said that "Several Christian radio and television stations and a lot of people were alerted."41 By appealing to Christian groups and the 8,000 subscribers to the Moral Concerns newsletter, a wave of letters, telegrams, and calls flooded the governor's office. "Five days before the veto, Timberlake and several state legislators presented their case against the measure to the governor and his staff."42 Following that meeting, a group composed of pastors and representatives of the American Life Lobby conducted a prayer rally at the Capitol; some 700 people were present for the rally. Thirteen days after receiving the bill on his desk, the governor announced his veto, saying "a person's sexual orientation should not be a basis for the establishment of a special protected class of individuals, especially in the absence of a compelling show of need." Assemblyman Agnos, a San Francisco Democrat who had fought for the legislation for eight years opined, "we were overwhelmed by opposition of what I call `the bigoted Bible thumpers.'"43

Bigoted Bible thumpers or not, the conservative, evangelical Christians had their way. Perhaps more importantly, the Christians gained their victory using a time-honored, acceptable method-- they brought political pressure to bear at the point of decision. It is no more, or no less than secular groups have been doing for a long time in America; the significance lies in the fact that the conservative, evangelical Christians have finally joined together, and there are lots of them.

As we have stated, the lines of battle are being drawn, the various sides are gathering their "mighty men" and planning their strategy of battle. From the statements of the T.V. preachers, we conclude that they believe that opposition to their belief in a great revival in America simply provides more fuel for the growing "fire of the Holy Spirit." As Jim Bakker of PTL would put it, "No weapon formed against us shall prosper."

PREACHING UNTIL THE END COMES: THE FUTURE
PROSPECTS OF TELEVANGELISM

PREACHING UNTIL THE END COMES: THE FUTURE PROSPECTS OF TELEVANGELISM

INTRODUCTION

But of that day and that hour knoweth
no man, no, not the angels which are in
heaven, neither the Son, but the Father.
Take ye heed, watch and pray: for ye
know not when the time is.

Mark 13:32-33

In the previous six chapters we have tried to describe, in broad outline, the societal events and changes that may have contributed to the rise of televangelism. We have also provided an analysis of the methods and techniques the T.V. preachers use in getting and keeping viewers, and a description of the "rising stars," "bright stars," and "guiding lights" of the electronic church. We have given attention to the breadth of Christian variety programming available to the viewers of Christian television; and finally, we have traced and described the involvement of conservative, evangelical Christians in the recent American political process. A main thesis throughout the book has been that the mainspring of increased

Christian activity is the electronic church-- Christian televangelism.

In this chapter we will ask, and provide our answer(s), to the most perilous question of all: What of the future of T.V. religion? We remind the reader of our previous statement in Chapter Two: "Social change is an on-going process and its effects make long-term forecasting about society difficult." This is not a prophetic book. What we propose to do in this chapter is give the reader our best, informed opinions in response to the question posed above.

REVIVAL AND RENEWAL

O Timothy, keep that which is committed
to thy trust, avoiding profane and vain
babblings, and oppositions of science
falsely so called: Which some professing
have erred concerning the faith. Grace
be with thee. Amen.

I Timothy 6:20-21

It seems to us that if the current religious revival, and the growth and expansion of Christian television is to continue, fundamentalists, evangelicals, pentecostals, and others must somehow manage to overcome the common societal conception that their position is not only simple, but that it is not profound. The staying power of the religious revival and, hence, T.V. religion, rests, we believe, on the ability of the movement's leaders to discredit the belief that to be an intellectual is to be politically and religiously liberal.

William G. McLoughlin's work on revivals, awakenings, and reform is, in our opinion, particularly applicable to a discussion of the future of Christian television.1 In his work, McLoughlin discusses the impact of the various "Great Awakenings" on the development of culture and politics in America. According to McLoughlin, awakenings are "periods of cultural

172

revitalization that begin in a general crisis of beliefs and values and extend over a generation or so, during which time a profound reorientation in beliefs and values takes place."2 While a profound reorientation in beliefs and values may not have taken place, there can be little doubt that the television evangelists seek such a change in American society. This is one aspect of their ministries that the T.V. preachers make unabashedly clear.

According to Jerry Falwell:3

> To promote the necessity of turning America back to God, the "I Love America" Club was formed. . . . . These and other "I Love America" efforts focus on the need for America to claim God's promise in II Chronicles 7:14, "If my people, which are called by my name, shall humble themselves, and pray, and seek my face, and turn from their wicked ways; then will I hear from heaven, and will forgive their sin, and will heal their land."

The erosion of American policies and values is rather clear to Jimmy Swaggart:4

> One can't help but note the similarities between the policies of our national leaders and those of Nazi Germany.

In Jim Bakker's magazine, "Together," he makes a plea for money to complete a home designed to permit expectant mothers to have their babies rather than abort them:5

> The lives of unborn babies hang in the balance...we must complete the People That Love Home to be a haven for women who choose not to abort their babies. The home will begin to save babies the moment it's opened. . . . . Surely in America we have the right to stand up for life, and provide a place of life at Heritage USA.

Colonel Doner, founder and director of Christian Voice, a non-profit public information, Christian lobbying, and political action organization, expressed the following ideas:6

173

The fate of this country is in your hands. That seems weird to a lot of you, I know. But the 1984 elections are going to be lost to the secular humanists and the liberal radicals if we don't do something. It is up to the Christian community. You see, the conservatives, the Republicans, whoever they are out there are basically on our side, are going to get enough votes to make up about 45% of what is needed. But they are not going to go over the top. It will be up to us in our local districts in our country and our congressional districts to provide that extra one to six percent of the vote. YOU CAN DO IT.

It seems clear to us that the Mass Media Ministers desire to see a profound reorientation in American values and beliefs. So also, does President Ronald Reagan. When he spoke to the National Religious Broadcasters on the day after he announced his 1984 candidacy for President, he quoted Solomon: "Train up a child in the way he should go, and when he is old he will not depart from it."[7] That sounds to us like a plea to return to old, basic American values.

There have been three Great Awakenings in America's short history. The First Great Awakening, beginning about 1730 and running through 1760, predated and prepared the colonists for the American Revolution. The period of time roughly corresponding to 1800-1830 saw the Second Great Awakening romanticize the common man, and argue "for the perfectibility of human nature, thereby supplying a moral element to the claims of Jacksonian Democracy and the motive energy for the anti-slavery movement."[8] The Third Great Awakening (1890-1920) was an outgrowth of the rapid industrialization of the late nineteenth and early twentieth centuries. As James Wilson has commented, the Third Great Awakening was also a response to the "social violence and economic conflict" that was associated with industrialization.[9] Wilson goes on to say that the ideological arguments of the Third Great Awakening were "fought out in the struggle between evangelical fundamentalism" on the one hand, and "the Social Gospel of Walter Rauschenbusch and the Protestant Progressives," on the other hand.[10] As most are aware, the Social Gospel, particularly as it was embodied in the "New Deal", prevailed and excerised a

174

great influence on American social, religious, and political thought.

The first three Great Awakenings had several common characteristics. Rapid social change is one attribute. Established values and moral conduct no longer seemed to correspond. Basic support institutions no longer seemed legitimate. Significant changes in family life and experimentation with new forms of marital living represent a second characteristic. This was particularly in response to the need to move to urban areas during the industrialization of America. A third factor relates to a generalized increase in violent crime and disruption of the public order. These same factors-- conflict between values and behavior, alienation from basic institutions, changes in traditional family forms, and an increase in violence and public acceptance of it, have been with us since the 1960's. They have led, as we commented in Chapter One, to a lonely individualism in American society. These conditions are the very "stuff" of religious revivals; and, we are squarely in the midst of such a revival today. We may very well be on the brink of, or perhaps well into, a Fourth Great Awakening in the United States. As Wilson has accurately pointed out, Great Awakenings have always been preceeded by religious revivals, and we know of no religious scholars, academics, or major news services that would doubt the authenticity of the current revival. The overriding question is its staying power and, equally important, it consequences. We will not pretend to answer the latter question, but we will attempt to address the staying power of the current revival, and the part that Christian television will play in it.

ON STAYING THE RACE

Know ye not that they which run in a
race run all, but one receiveth the
prize? So run, that ye may obtain.
And every man that striveth for the
mastery is temperate in all things.
Now they do it to obtain a corruptible
crown; but we an incorruptible.

175

I Corinthians 9:24-25

Religion, particularly evangelical Christianity, is on the rise in America. Not only is interest in evangelism on the increase, it is no longer restricted to pentecostal, charasmatic, or holiness faiths. Mainline churches, many of which eschewed evangelism to emphasize social ethics in the `60's and `70's, are making plans to carry out the great commission through evangelical activities. The new attention to evangelism in mainline churches has come so far that according to Grady Allison, program director for evangelism for the Presbyterian Church (USA), "You can even talk about evangelism in polite circles of society."11

What turned the attention of the mainline churches away from social ethics and toward evangelism? In just two words, declining membership. Declining membership encouraged the mainliners to become more interested in church growth, and evangelism is the time-honored way to accomplish church growth. The mainliners are interested in evangelism; however, it is unlikely that Methodists, Presbyterians, Lutherans, Episcopalians, and other mainline members would be comfortable in doing traditional "confrontational evangelism." Confrontational evangelism has a long history in religious fundamentalism, and involves door-to-door visitation and witnessing, asking people to make a decision for Jesus and to join the Body of Christ. Clearly, middle and upper-middle class Protestants are not likely to enjoy, and participate in such activities. But there is a new form of evangelism that is more compatable with the mainline churches-- it can be called "process" or "friendship" evangelism. It is gaining in popularity as a evangelizing technique to foster church growth. Process, or friendship evangelism interprets a "decision" for Christ as only the first step in the process of being converted and becoming a responsible church member. In essence, friendship evangelism involves witnessing to a network of friends, neighbors, or family members, over a period of time, often extending across many years. According to Christianity Today:12

> Win Arn and Charles Arn, of the Church Growth Institute, have asked over 14,000 lay people the question, "What or who was responsible for

your coming to Christ and your church." Less than 10 percent credit a pastor, a visitation program, or an evangelistic crusade. Between 75 percent and 90 percent say they owe their Christian faith to a friend or a relative.

The evidence suggests, therefore, that process or friendship evangelism is a more gentle, subtle, and reassuring method to gain converts than is the traditional confrontational approach. What process evangelism does more effectively than confrontational evangelism is to get, and keep, the convert in church. The friendship approach not only gains converts, but yields "fruit that will last."

If evangelism is growing in our society (and it is), the T.V. preachers should be a part of its growth. However, the T.V. preachers rely on a para-confrontational approach to making the religious decision. Current data suggest that converts gained through the traditional confrontational approach usually do not become active, responsible members of a local church. This is certainly true over the long haul. Of course, the Mass Media Ministers, especially Pat Robertson and Jim Bakker, might argue that they employ a kind of "friendship" evangelism by coming into the new converts home each day to reaffirm and reestablish the believer's decision for Christ. They might also suggest that they encourage their viewers to join and participate in what they call a local, full gospel church. In fact, Robertson and Bakker claim to have linked-up with pastors all over America whom they will be happy to send to call on the new convert. According to Bakker's Together magazine:13

> Not only does PTL provide telephone counseling, but the PTL Pastor Follow-up ministry coordinates a staff of over 6,000 pastors and laymen across the nation (from many evangelical denominations) who visit new converts and/or provide personal counseling for those who make this request. Church information is also provided for those desiring to become established in a local church. Last year, over 30,000 contacts were made by PTL Follow-up pastors in their areas.

It is instructive, we believe, that Bakker's PTL Pastor Follow-up ministry only visits those new

convert's "who make this request." Furtheremore, church
information is provided only "for those desiring to
become established in a local church." It seems to us,
therefore, that no matter how many "contacts" are made
by "follow-up pastors," what the T.V. preachers offer
as evangelism is a poor substitute for even the
confrontational approach. In addition, reliable data
confirm that the overwhelming majority of those who
watch Christian television are already converted,
believing, and practicing Christians. As far as we
know, the Robert H. Schuller Institute for Successful
Church Leadership is the only program offered by a T.V.
preacher to instruct pastors in gaining new converts to
their churches. If Christian television is going to
experience continued growth, the T.V. preachers must
recognize that most of their faithful are already
believers and begin to direct their ministries, at
least in part, toward working more closely with laymen,
pastors, and other church leaders in assuring that
converts become responsible church members and
participants.

RELIGIOUS BROADCASTING: THE TRUMPET OF THE LORD

The second woe is past; and, behold, the
third woe cometh quickly. And the seventh
angel sounded; and there were great voices
in heaven, saying, The kingdoms of this
world are become the kingdoms of our Lord,
and of his Christ; and he shall reign for
ever and ever.

Revelation 11:14-15

    Religious broadcasting has been, and continues to be,
a mighty trumpet of the Lord. As a result of
television, the sound of the mighty trumpet is being
heard throughout the world, even unto the ends of the
earth. As Jim Bakker is fond of saying, he believes
that we are in the "end times" because for the first
time in history Christians have the means--
televisions, computers, satellites, and other
technology to fulfill the "great commission" and "bring

Jesus back." If nothing else, Christian television can lay claim to justification by prophecy.

But Christian television and the T.V. preachers can claim much more than justification by prophecy. In America, religious broadcasting has spawned many parachurch ministries and has been responsible for popularizing new ways of getting out the religious message through other forms of mass media. Perhaps more importantly, Christian television provided a vehicle through which evangelicals could develop a national, common sense of self. In fact, through the various international television ministries, evangelicals are coming to identify with their foreign neighbors. What all of this means, at least in part, is that evangelicals across America are hearing the same message and beginning to recognize its implications: "we are one in the Lord and we are strong in the power of his might."14

RELIGIOUS PROGRAMMING: ACCOMMODATION OR CONFRONTATION?

And I saw a great white throne, and him
that sat on it, from whose face the earth
and the heaven fled away; and there was
found no place for them. And I saw the
dead, small and great, stand before God;
and the books were opened: and another
book was opened, which is the book of life:
and the dead were judged out of those
things which were written in the books,
according to their works. And the sea gave
up the dead which were in it; and death and
hell delivered up the dead which were in
them; and they were judged every man
according to their works.

Revelation 20|11-13

If Christian radio and television has done anything, it has grown. Today, Christian radio stations number in the thousands, and television stations number over 50;

and, of course, Trinity Broadcasting Network (TBN), Christian Broadcasting Network (CBN), and The Inspirational Network (PTL), blanket the nation with religious broadcasting. The proliferation of broadcast stations and satellite networks has not, however, been without its associated problems. High on the list of problems is the area of program content. An important question centers on just how many Christian talk shows (featuring up-beat "you can succeed" messages, bright-eyed, rosy cheeked youths, celebrity guests, pop-gospel music, testimonials, and endless pleas for money), the viewing audience can tolerate. Are there limits to the number of Bible prophecy shows folks can be enticed to watch? And what about teaching shows-- how many analyses of giving and receiving, healing, spiritual gifts, or forgiveness do viewers need, or more importantly, how much do they want? If fresh program content and new formats are not devised, T.V. religion may find itself suffering from the primary difficulty of secular television: a lot of air time to fill, and insufficient quantities of ideas to creatively fill it. If they are not careful, the religious broadcasters could wind-up giving America a Christian version of television mediocrity-- a sort of T.V. gospel glut.

The outcomes just mentioned could be even worse than imagined if, as reported in Christianity Today, a world Christian Consortium actualizes on its plans to launch the first of three Christian satellites by 1985.15 As reported by Bisset, "the first satellite will broadcast to North and South America, the second to Europe and Africa, the third to Asia and the Pacific."16 Bisset goes on to say that each satellite "will have its alloted 24 television channels plus 24 FM subchannels." Imagine the saturation effect of 24 additional satellite channels of Christian television broadcasting to North America, and a total of 72 additional channels throughout the world! The possibility of so much religious programming creating a sort of "gospel boredom" may threaten the viability of the current "bright stars" of T.V. religion. Of course, there is also the possibility that an explosion of religious T.V. channels could successfully evangelize the world.

Regardless of whether additional Christian satellites are orbiting in space, religious broadcasting has, in fact, come of age. As Bisset has argued, however, Christian television and its "bright stars" still face

some important challenges.17 Bisset breaks the
challenges down into four categories: (1) technology,
(2) reaching non-viewers,(3) adressing current issues,
and (4) program content. We have already discussed
program content, so we will turn our attention to the
other three categories mentioned by Bisset.

Technology.

   The principle problem associated with technology is
the fact that technological breakthroughs and advances
are occuring at a "future shock" rate. Consider just
some of the evidence: cable and pay television now
abound; videocasette recorders are fast finding their
way into American homes; and, videodiscs already make
it possible for bookstores to sell T.V. programs,
concerts, and revival meetings, at affordable prices
to the general public. For the T.V. preachers, however,
using available technology without being used by it, to
the detriment of sending the religious message, may be
the greatest challenge that they face today. Becoming
and being a "bright star" of Christian television is a
"heady" experience, and no one ever accused the
well-known T.V. preachers of having inadequate images
of themselves. The desire to keep one's "star" status
may breed competition rather than cooperation. The T.V.
preachers are, after all, human. They may be "men of
God," but emphasis should be properly placed on the
word "men" in the phrase "men of God." How religious
broadcasters use the opportunities that advancing
technology presents them will determine, in large
measure, how glorious their future will be.

Current Issues.

   According to Bisset, the T.V. preachers must fulfill
their "responsibility to speak prophetically as well as
scripturally to current issues."18 Christian
evangelicals have made a name for themselves through
their recent participation in the political process in
America. The T.V. preachers, especially Jerry Falwell,
have spoken out on a number of issues, primarily those
issues they are against. Politically, they are
anti-abortion, anti-pronography, anti-homosexuality,
anti-nuclear freeze, anti-defense spending cuts,
anti-scientific evolutionism, anti-ERA, anti-secular
humanism, and anti-divorce. Bisset congratulates such

activists "who have forced America's leaders to recognize and respect the majority of the electorate who adhere to Judeo-Christian moral values."19 We do not know where Bisset gets his data, but we are unconvinced that the "majority" of those who adhere to the Judeo-Christian moral tradition subscribe to all of the evangelical "anti" positions.

While we disagree with Bisset's claim that the majority' of the electorate agree with the televangelists, we do agree that religious broadcasting could become, if not careful, "synonymous with a certain political philosophy."20 In fact, we believe that many T.V. preachers have already been so labeled by the general public. It is certain that there are issues in this country that the televangelists could address that would move them more into the mainstream of late 20th century America. For example, the T.V. preachers could speak to the problem of hundreds of thousands of hungry people in America, to discrimination because of sex, race, or age, to the continuing problem of unemployment, to the many uncurable/crippling diseases, to overcrowding in America's prisons, to increasing illiteracy, or to the problem of starving people all over the world. It seems to us that if the T.V. preachers could find a methodology through which they could speak, in a positive way, to the current issues of today without compromising their gospel message, many middle-class Americans might be attracted to their ministries. It is here, in the rhetoric of the message, that the T.V. preachers face yet another challenge.

The Disinterested Viewer.

The overwhelming majority of Americans do not watch Christian television, and the majority of those who do watch religious broadcasting are those who are already converted, believing followers of Christ. The American Heritage Dictionary of the English Language defines broadcasting as "to make known over a wide area," or "to sow (seed) over a wide area." If we accept this definition of broadcasting, then Christian television has clearly been engaged in successful broadcasting of the gospel message. If, however, we impose the requirement that "a wide area" means a wide audience reaching a representative cross section of the population, then religious broadcasting would have to be called religious "narrowcasting." The most significant problem facing the T.V. preachers today is the fact that they have failed to devise methods to bring the millions of disinterested viewers to their programs. If they do not find some way to entice the unconcerned members of the viewing public, the T.V. preachers may soon discover the limits of their audience size.

The pressing question, of course, is how to broaden the appeal and attraction of the ministries of the T.V. preachers. One answer (and perhaps the most viable one), has already been provided: T.V. preachers must find a way to discredit the image that they believe that to be an intellectual is to be politically and religiously liberal. We are impressed with the fact that open hostility seems to be shown by most T.V. preachers when they speak of the "radical/liberal," "anti-prayer/anti-God," "pro-abortion/pro-homosexual," people in America. Usually, all of these descriptions are applied, willy nilly, to all people who do not agree with their positions. We fail to see why the T.V. preachers feel they must criticize, demean, abhor, and attack the vast majority of American citizens who live, work, and worship in the mainstream of American cultural life. By mixing the religious with the cultural and political, and then claiming the singular righteousness of their own position, the T.V. preachers do more to alienate than they do to accommodate the rest of their world.

America is built upon the diversification of ideologies, and to insist on a unitary point of view runs counter to what is deeply rooted in the consciousness of America. Religious pluralism is not only a fact, it has become a part of the "American Creed." We agree with Bisset that if the televangelists are to continue to grow they must squarely and honestly address their "responsibility to present the gospel with clarity and relevance."21 Bisset goes on to say:22

> The listening and viewing public of the future-- Christian as well as secular-- will be more critical than audiences of the past 25 years. Simple solutions to complex problems will not easily win a hearing, nor will truisms and cliches.

Failure to recognize and carry out this obligation will result in the ultimate failure of televangelism to carry out "the great commission."

We closed Chapter Two by saying that we have no way of assessing the veracity of the T.V. preachers. Now, as we come to the close of the book, we reaffirm that earlier conclusion. In the process of spending hour upon hour watching the T.V. preachers we have, of course, formed our own opinions about the motives and veracity of individual Mass Media Ministers. Nevertheless, we still assert that we have been unable to discover a reliable and/or valid litmus test to evaluate the integrity of the T.V. preachers. Again, we have our own personal assessments of the various television preachers-- some make us suspect, some make us angry, and some make us think they are using the gospel message for personal gain. Some, of course, make us listen attentively.

Aside from the question of their veracity, is the fact that the T.V. preachers are reaching millions of people in America and around the world. While the personal motives of the T.V. preachers are important, the effect of the T.V. evangelism is equally, or perhaps more important. Christian television, i.e., electronic evangelism, is a relatively new phenomenon in the modern world. It has come a surprising distance in a short period of time. We do not know just how far it will go.

However, given the success the T.V. preachers have enjoyed thus far, we believe they will find new and innovative ways to address the problems that currently face religious broadcasting and that Christian television will become an even mightier "trumpet of the Lord."

The T.V. preachers are not going to disappear from the American television scene. The established television preachers are here to stay, and more are on the way. The best we can do for those who watch Christian television is to offer the caution of Jesus in Matthew 24:4 when he spoke of the Coming of False Christs:

"Take heed that no man deceive you."

184

AFTERWORD

The Reverend John H. Loving
Grace Episcopal Church
Ponca City, OK

AFTERWORD
The Reverend John H. Loving

As pastor in one of the "mainline" Churches, I have had over the years a `knee-jerk' reaction to the Electronic Church and its superstars that might easily be anticipated: resentment at their success, suspicion of their motives, incredulity of their stated numbers, envy of their finances, and condescension toward their theology and Biblical literalism. Yet Professor Cardwell in this penetrating study has clearly demonstrated the self-defeating and premature nature of this reaction. Here is a scholar, a sociologist, an avid chronicler of religious commitment and behavior who has spent literally hundreds of hours observing these men and women at work, visiting their headquarters, comparing their preaching styles, their backgrounds, their respective emphases. He not only watches their programs, he enters their world, and sees their potential as well as their foibles.

What comes across to me from this fascinating narrative is a word of judgement on the mainline Churches. The Electronic Church succeeds primarily where we have failed. Our pastoral ministeries have been in large measure confined to a few parishioners, leaving vast numbers of aged, infirm, and confined individuals groping for sympathetic companionship, personal faith, and a sense of God's abiding presence. What a wonderful challenge to the lay ministry of the Church: telephone ministries, nursing home ministries, birthday and holiday greetings, and so on. We have also ignored or played down the importance of modern, computerized audio-visual technology, leaving the field of "Christian television" by and large in the hands of a minority, which is no longer such a minority! Furthermore, in many instances preaching has become perfunctory, glib, tangential to Holy Scripture, and unrelated to the needs and questions of those in the congregation. Is it any wonder that the vacuum has been filled by those who speak with power and conviction and who call forth a response from their hearers?

The Church's Biblical and sacramental ministry of healing has been ignored and in its place has arisen a sensationalist phenomenon that often focuses more on the "healer" than on divine grace. Furthermore, the Churches' well-intentioned efforts to work for justice and sustenance for the hungry and dispossessed have often been carried out despite the opposition and prejudices of the men and women in the pews. Many of these people are among those who have subsequently voted with their feet and withheld their dollars. Finally, we have failed to challenge our members to support financially the missionary thrust and ongoing work of Christs' Church and thereby have failed to bring them to commit themselves and their resources to God's Kingdom. Thus our outreach has been stymied, our educational program has suffered, salaries have fallen behind, and many churches have tragically fallen victim to a defensive, survivalist attitude. Surely, this is not the vision toward which God is calling his Church!

To see the problems and to perceive God's judgement through them is not necessarily to subscribe to the apparently simplistic solutions suggested by some of the spokesmen for the Electronic Church. But if they can help us see ourselves, they have indeed fulfilled a

188

prophetic role and we should thank God for them.

In conclusion, as Professor Cardwell suggests, there is the possibility that in God's good time we may be given the chance to work together as stewards and servants of God to proclaim His Glory, to sing His praises, to be nurtured by His sacraments, and to serve the hungry, the oppressed, the outcasts of society in the spirit of the Son of Man.

> "He hath showed you, O Man, what is good;
> and what doth the Lord require of thee
> but to do justice, and to love kindness,
> and to walk humbly with thy God?"

Micah 6:8

NOTES

NOTES

CHAPTER ONE

1. Jerry D. Cardwell, The Social Context of Religiosity, Wash., D.C.: University Press of America, 1980.

2. See, for example: Ronald L. Johnstone, Religion in Society, 2nd. ed., Englewood Cliffs, N.J.: Prectice-Hall, Inc., 1983.

3. Joseph Fichter, Social Relations in the Urban Parish, Chicago: University of Chicago Press, 1954.

4. Allen Spitzer, "Religious Structure in Mexico," Alpha Kappa Deltan, Winter, 1960, pp. 54-58.

5. Glenn M. Vernon, "An Inquiry into the Scalability of Church Orthodoxy," Sociology and Social Research, 39:5, May-June, 1955, pp. 324-327; Charles Y. Glock, "The Sociology of Religion," in Sociology Today, Robert K. Merton, ed., New York: Basic Books, 1959, pp. 167-169

6. Glenn M. Vernon and Jerry D. Cardwell, "Males, Females, and Religion," in The Social Context of Religiosity, Jerry D. Cardwell, ed., Wash. D.C.: University Press of America, 1980, pp. 75-110.

7. Glenn M. Vernon, The Sociology of Religion, New York: McGraw-Hill Book Co., 1962.

8. Glenn M. Vernon, "The Religious `Nones': A Neglected Category," Journal for the Scientific Study of Religion, 7, Fall, 1968, pp. 219-229.

9. Glenn M. Vernon, "Types of Religion: Religion in 4-T," in Types and Dimensions of Religion, G.M. Vernon, ed., Salt Lake City: Association for the Study of Religion, 1972, pp. 1-18.

10. Ibid.

11. Glenn M. Vernon, "The Religious `Nones': A Neglected Category," Journal for the Scientific Study of Religion, 7, Fall, 1968, pp. 219-229.

193

12.   Gerhard Lenski, The Religious Factor, Garden City, N.Y.: Doubleday, 1961; Jerry D. Cardwell, "The Relationship between Religious Commitment and Attitudes Toward Premarital Sexual Permissiveness: A 5-D Analysis," Sociological Analysis, 30:2, Summer, 1969, pp. 13-25; Howard J. Ruppel, "Religiosity and Premarital Sexual Permissiveness: A Response to the Reiss-Heltsley and Broderick Debate," Journal of Marriage and the Family, 1970, pp. 647-655; Stephen L. Finner and J. D. Gamache, "The Relation Between Religious Commitment and Attitudes Toward Induced Abortion," Sociological Analysis, 30:1, Spring, 1969, 1-12.

13.   N. J. Demerath III and Richard Levinson, "On Baiting the Dissident Hook: The Methodology of Religious Belief," unpublished paper, 1967, cited in N. J. Demerath and Phillip Hammond, Religion in Social Context, New York: Random House, 1969, p. 123.

14.   Peter Benson and Bernard Spilka, "God Image as a Function of Self Esteem and Locus of Control," Journal for the Scientific Study of Religion, 12:3, September, 1973, pp. 297-310.

15.   Demerath and Hammond, p. 123.

16.   Jerry D. Cardwell, "On the Theory of Multidimensional Religiosity," unpublished doctoral dissertation, University of Utah, 1972.

17.   Robert Alston, "Review of the Polls," Journal for the Scientific Study of Religion," 12:3, September, 1973, pp. 349-351.

18.   Donald R. Ploch, "Religion as an Independent Variable: A Critique of Some Major Research," in Changing Perspectives in the Scientific Study of Religion, Allen W. Eister, ed., New York: John Wiley and Sons, 1974, pp. 275-294.

19.   Ibid.

20.   Paul Tillich, Dynamics of Faith, New York: Harper Torchbooks, 1957.

21.   Richmond Times-Dispatch, April, 1979, p. 33.

22.   Thomas F. O'Dea, The Sociology of Religion,
Englewood Cliffs, N.J.: Prentice-Hall, Inc., 1962.

23.   Rodney Stark,   "Comment: On Buying Back Youthful
Daubings," Sociological Analysis, 41:2, Summer, 1980,
p. 162.

24. Ibid., p. 163.

25.   Peter L. Berger, The Heretical Imperative, Garden
City, N.Y.: Doubleday, 1978.

26.   Jackson W. Carroll, Douglas W. Johnson, and Martin
E. Marty, Religion in America, New York: Harper and
Row, 1979, p. 6.

27. Ibid.

28.   David   Riesman,   cited in George T. Harris,
"Spiritual   Terror   in   the   Ecstatic   Eighties,"
Introduction to Jeffrey K. Hadden and Charles W. Swann,
Prime Time Preachers, Reading, Mass.: Addison-Wesley,
1981, xix.

29.   George T. Harriss, "Spiritual Terror in the
Ecstatic Eighties," Introduction to Jeffrey K. Hadden
and Charles E. Swann, Prime Time Preachers, Reading,
Mass.: Addison-Wesley, 1981, pp. xiii-xxi.

30. Ibid, p. xix.

31. Ibid, p. xix.

32. Ibid, p. xix.

33. Will Herberg, Protestant-Catholic-Jew, Garden City,
N.J.: Doubleday, 1955.

34. Ibid, p. 12.

35. Carrol, Johnson, and Marty, Religion in America.

36.   Jeffrey K. Hadden and Charles E. Swann, Prime Time
Preachers, Reading, Mass.: Addison-Wesley, 1981.

37.   Ben Armstrong, The Electric Church. Nashville:
Thomas Nelson Publishers, 1979.

38. Ronald L. Johnstone, Religion in Society, Englewood Cliffs, N.J.: Prentice-Hall, Inc., 1983, p. 116.

39. Ibid.

40. Reported in Hadden and Swann, Prime Time Preachers, 1981, p. 35.

41. The Evangelist, Special Edition, Vol. 15, No. 11, 1983.

42. Ibid.

43. Jerry Falwell Ministries, "We've Come this Far by FAITH," 1981, p. 50.

CHAPTER TWO

1. Jackson W. Carroll, D.W. Johnson, and Martin E. Marty, Religion in America: 1950 to the Present. New York: Harper and Row, 1979.

2. Cited in Carroll, Johnson, and Marty, 1979, p. 60.

3. Jeffrey K. Hadden and Charles E. Swann, Prime Time Preachers, Reading, Mass.: Addison-Wesley, 1981.

4. Will Herberg, Protestant, Catholic, Jew. Garden City, New Jersey: Doubleday, 1955.

5. T. George Harris, "Spiritual Terror in the Ecstatic Eighties," in the Introduction to Prime Time Preachers, Jeffrey K. Hadden and Charles E. Swann, Reading, Mass.: Addison-Wesley, 1981.

6. Newsweek, "Swaggart's one-edged sword," January 9, 1984, p. 65.

7. Newsweek, "Swaggart's one-edged sword," January 9, 1984, p. 65.

8. Jerry D. Cardwell, "Church Attendance and Perceived Powerlessness," in The Social Context of Religiosity, J. D. Cardwell, (ed.), Washington D.C.: University Press of America, 1980.

CHAPTER THREE

1. Jerry D. Cardwell, The Social Context of Religiosity, Washington, D.C.: University Press of America, 1980.

2. Jerry D. Cardwell and Glenn M. Vernon, "Males, Females, and Religion," in The Social Context of Religiosity, J.D. Cardwell (ed.)., Wash., D.C.: University Press of America, 1980, Chapter 4.

3. Ibid.

4. Ibid.

5. Ibid.

6. Newsweek, "Inspirational Romances," February 20, 1984, p. 69.

7. Jeffrey K. Hadden and Charles E. Swann, Prime Time Preachers, Reading, Mass.: Addison-Wesley, 1981, pp. 61-62.

8 Jim Bakker, "How to Have an Abundant Harvest," Together, January/February, 1983, pp. 24, 25.

CHAPTER FOUR

1. Rex Humbard, To Tell The World, Englewood Cliffs, N.J.: Prentice-Hall, 1977.

2. Ibid.

3. Jeffrey K. Hadden and Charles E. Swann, Prime Time Preachers. Reading, Mass.: Addison-Wesley, 1981.

4. Jim Bakker, Together Magazine, "The PTL Story," January/February, 1983, p. 8.

5. Jim Bakker, Together Magazine, "The PTL Story," January/February, 1983, p.8.

6. Jim Bakker, Together Magazine, "The PTL Story," January/February, 1983, p.8.

7. Jim Bakker, Together Magazine, "The PTL Story," January/February, 1983, p. 8.

8. Christianity Today, "PTL: Please Toss a Lifesaver," April, 1979, pp. 41-42.

9. Christianity Today, "PTL: Please Toss a Lifesaver," April, 1979, pp. 41-42.

10. Christianity Today, "Bakker Turns in his Apron after the PTL Cake Falls," May, 1979, pp. 44-45.

11. Hadden and Swann, Prime Time Preachers, 1981, p. 35.

12. Ibid.

13. Paula Span, "Robert Schuller: The Best Selling Televangelist, The Wall Street Journal, Thursday, May 3, 1984, p. 20.

14. Paula Span, "Robert Schuller: The Best Selling Televangelist, The Wall Street Journal, Thursday, May 3, 1984, p. 20.

15. Paula Span, "Robert Schuller: The Best Selling Televangelist, The Wall Street Journal, Thursday, May 3, 1984, p. 20.

CHAPTER FIVE

1. The "Times Arrow," Vol 5, No 3, March/April, 1983, p. 19.

2. Jim Bakker, PTL Satellite Network Brochure.

3. The Saturday Evening Post, "Biggest Bargain in Family Vacation in Dixieland," May/June, 1982, p. 80.

4. The Saturday Evening Post, "Biggest Bargain in Family Vacation in Dixieland," May/June, 1982, p. 80.

CHAPTER SIX

1. Richard V. Pierard, "Reagan and the Evangelicals:

The Making of a Love Affair," The Christian Century, December 21-28, 1983, p. 1183.

2.   Richard V.   Pierard, "Reagan and the Evangelicals: The Making of a Love Affair," The Christian Century, December 21-28, 1983, p. 1183.

3.   Richard V.   Pierard, "Reagan and the Evangelicals: The Making of a Love Affair," The Christian Century, December 21-28, 1983, p. 1183.

4.   Richard V.   Pierard, "Reagan and the Evangelicals: The Making of a Love Affair," The Chrisitan Century, December 21-28, 1983, p. 1183.

5.   Richard V.   Pierard, "Reagan and the Evangelicals: The Making of a Love Affair," The Christian Century, December 21-28, 1983, p. 1183.

6.   Richard V.   Pierard, "Reagan and the Evangelicals: The Making of a Love Affair," The Christian Century, December 21-28, 1983, p. 1183.

7.   Jeffrey K. Hadden and Charles E. Swann, Prime Time Preachers,   Reading,   Mass.:   Addison-Wesley,   1981; Richard V.   Pierard, "Reagan and the Evangelicals: The Making of a Love Affair," The Christian Century, December 21-28, 1983; Louise J. Lorentzen, "Evangelical Life Style Concerns Expressed in Political Action," Sociological Analysis, 41, 2, Summer, 1980, 144-154.

8.   Cited in Pierard, "Reagan and the Evangelicals: The Making of a Love Affair," p. 1184.

9. Ibid., p. 1184.

10. Ibid., p. 1184.

11.   "A   Tide   of   Born-Again   Politics,"   Newsweek, September 15, 1980, p. 36.

12.   "Reagan Stirs the Broadcasters with an Evangelical Speech," Christianity Today, April 6, 1984, p. 39.

13.   "Reagan Stirs the Broadcasters with an Evangelical Speech," Christianity Today, April 6, 1984, p. 39.

14. Ibid., p. 39.

15. Ibid., pp. 39-40.

16. Ibid., p. 39.

17. "Once Again, Reagan Pitches for Evangelical Support," Christianity Today, April 6, 1984, pp. 61.

18. Ibid.

19. "A Tide of Born-Again Politics," Newsweek, September 15, 1980, p. 28.

20. "We've Come this Far by FAITH," Jerry Falwell Ministries, 1981, p. 50.

21. Ibid.

22. Ibid.

23. "A Tide of Born-Again Politics," Newsweek, September 15, 1980, p. 30.

24. Ibid., p. 24.

25. Anson Shupe and William A. Stacy, Born Again Politics and the Moral Majority: What the Social Surveys Really Show. New York: The Edwin Mellen Press, 1982.

26. Edward P. Freeland, review of Shupe and Stacy, "Born Again Politics and the Moral Majority: What the Social Surveys Really Show," Journal for the Scientific Study of Religion, Vo. 23, No. 1, March 1984, p. 96.

27. Ibid.

28. Ibid.

29. Ted Pantaleo, The Freedom Report, Vol. 2, No. 2, 1984.

30. Letter from Pat Robertson, April 5, 1984.

31. Ted Pantaleo, The Freedom Report, Vo. 2, No. 2, 1984.

32. Ibid.

33. Ibid.

34. "A Tide of Born-Again Politics," Newsweek, September 15, 1980, pp. 29-30.

35. Cited in Jeffrey K. Hadden and Charles E. Swann, Prime Time Preachers, Reading, Mass.: Addison-Wesley, 1981, p. 50.

36. U. S. News and World Report, "When Church and State Collide," March 5, 1984.

37. U. S. News, Ibid.

38. Ibid. 39. U. S. News and World Report, "Religion is Again a Potent Social Force," March 5, 1984.

40. Christianity Today, "Christian Activists Help Kill A California Gay Rights Bill," April 20, 1984, p. 42,

41. Ibid., p. 41.

42. Ibid.

43. Ibid.

CHAPTER SEVEN

1. William G. McLoughlin, Revivals, Awakenings, and Reform. Chicago: University of Chicago Press, 1978.

2. Ibid.

3. Jerry Falwell Ministries, "We've Come This Far By FAITH," 1981, pp. 39-40.

4. Jimmy Swaggart, "Abortion: America's Greatest Crime," The Evangelist, (Special Edition), Vol. 15, No. 11, p. 6.

5. Jim Bakker, "We MUST Complete This Home...Now!," Together, May/June, 1984, p. 20.

6. Colonel Doner, "Voter Registration in the Church," Times Arrow, Vol. 15, No. 3, March/April, 1984, p. 14.

7. "Reagan Stirs the Broadcasters with an Evangelical Speech," Christianity Today, March, 1984, p. 40.

8.   James   Q. Wilson, "Reagan and the Republican
Revival," Commentary, October, 1980, pp. 25-32.

9. Ibid., p. 29.

10. Ibid., p. 29.

11. Tim Stafford, "Evangelism: The New Wave is a Tidal
Wave," Christianity Today, May 18, 1984, p. 43.

12. Ibid., p. 63.

13.   Jim Bakker, Together, January/February, 1983, p.
26.

14. Tom Bisset, "Religious Broadcasting Comes of Age,"
Christianity Today, September 4, 1984, p. 33.

15. Ibid., p. 35.

16. Ibid.

17. Ibid.

18. Tom Bisset, "Religious Broadcasting Comes of Age,"
Christianity Today, September 4, 1984, p. 35.

19. Ibid.

20. Ibid.

21. Ibid.

22. Tom Bisset, "Religious Broadcasting Comes of Age,"
Christianity Today, September 4, 1984, p. 35.

Humbard, Rex, 22, 30, 33, 66, 78, 91, 94-97 197
Humbard, Maude Aimee, 96

[I]

I Love America rallies, 157
Inspirational Network, the, (see PTL)
Internalization of religious commitment,
     the, 39-41

[J]

Jews, comments on, 43
Johnson, D. W., 28, 195n, 196n
Johnstone, Ronald, 193n, 195n

[K]

Khoemni, Ayatollah, 29
Kinchlow, Ben, 35
King, Martin Luther, Jr., 38

[L]

Lenski, Gerhard, 194n
Levinson, Richard, 7
Levitt, Zola, xiii, 134-135
Lewis, Ann, 159
Lewis, David, 132
Lewis, Jerry Lee, 107

Liberty Baptist College, 99

Lorentzen, L., 199n
Loving, John, 185
Luther, Martin, 40, 46

[M]

McAteer, Ed., 158
McGovern, George, 156
McLoughlin, William, G., 172, 201
Marty, Martin, 28

Mass Media Members, creating and maintaining, 32-34

Merton, Robert K., 193n

Moral Majority, 155-160
      founding of, 156-157
      positions of, 50-51, 181
      methods of, 158-159
      analysis of, 159-160

Murdock, Mike, 136, 137

[N]

National Affairs Briefing (Dallas), 145, 150
National Association of Evangelicals (NAE),
      142-143
National Religious Broadcasters (NRB), 151-154
      composition of, 151-152
      Reagan and, 152-153

Nelson, Gaylord, 156
Nielson, A.C., 23

[O]

O'Dea, Thomas F., 13, 195n

"Old Time Gospel Hour," 99

Otis, George, 147

Riesman, David, 19, 31, 195n

"Rising Stars," 121-131
     Bob Tilton, 122-125
     Kenneth Copeland, 125-128
     Jerry Savelle, 128-129
     James Robison, 129-131

Roberts, Oral, 22, 30, 46, 47, 66, 72, 78, 93-94,
115
Roberts, Richard, 47, 66, 94
Robertson, Pat, 5, 22, 30, 32, 39, 46, 51, 52, 55, 57,
66, 78, 80, 91, 95, 97, 108-112, 141, 150, 151, 161,
162, 165, 166, 200n
Robison. James, 42, 43, 78, 95, 120, 129
Rogers, Roy, 55

Roman Catholicism, comments on, 43

Ruppel, Howard, 194n

[S]

Savelle, Jerry, 66, 120, 128-129
Schuller, Robert, 65, 78, 112-116, 178

Secular Humanism, 183

Shupe, Anson, 159, 160, 200n

Social change, 12
     and religion, 12-13

Span, Paula, 114, 115, 198n
Spilka, Bernard, 7, 194n
Spitzer, Allen, 3, 193n
Stacy, W.A., 159, 200n
Stafford, Tim, 202n
Stark, Rodney, 15, 16, 195n
Sumrall, Lester, 66, 133-134

Supreme Court, 164

Sutton, Hilton, 165

Swaggart, Jimmy, 22, 23, 30, 32, 42, 43, 50, 66, 78, 80, 91, 95, 105-108, 115, 119, 121, 201n
Swann, Charles, 22, 31, 68, 110, 120, 147, 195n, 196n, 197n, 198n, 199n, 201n

[T]

Thomas, Cal, 159
Thomas, W.I., 59
Tillich, Paul, 10, 194n
Tilton, Bob, 120, 122-125
Tilton, Marte, 122-125
Timberlake, W.B., 167, 168
Toffler, Alvin, 12

Trinity Broadcasting Network (TBN), 101
T.V. preachers, veracity of, 58-59

[U]

U.S. Congress, 177

[V]

VanderMaten, Bob, 137, 138
Vernon, Glenn, 5, 22, 44, 193n, 197n

Viewers of Christian television, 63-82
    number of, 22-23
    gender of, 65-68
    age of, 68-72
    education of, 72-76
    region of residence, 76-78

[W]

Wesley, John, 40
Weyrich, Paul, 149, 158
Wilson, James Q., 174, 175, 202n

WANX, television, 43
WLIV, television, 43

Wozniak, Paul R., v.

ABOUT THE AUTHOR

Jerry D. Cardwell is professor of sociology and Head, Department of Sociology, Anthropology, and Social Work, Western Kentucky University, Bowling Green, Ky. He is the vice-president of The Society for the Study of Symbolic Interaction. He has published a number of articles on religious commitment and has authored several books, including THE SOCIAL CONTEXT OF RELIGIOSITY.